An Analysis of

Friedrich Schleiermacher's

On Religion: Speeches to its Cultured Despisers

Ruth Jackson

Published by Macat International Ltd
24:13 Coda Centre, 189 Munster Road, London SW6 6AW.

Distributed exclusively by Routledge
2 Park Square, Milton Park, Abingdon, Oxon OX14 4RN
711 Third Avenue, New York, NY 10017, USA

Routledge is an imprint of the Taylor & Francis Group, an informa business

www.macat.com
info@macat.com

Cataloguing in Publication Data
A catalogue record for this book is available from the British Library.
Library of Congress Cataloguing-in-Publication Data is available upon request.
Cover illustration: Kim Thompson

ISBN 978-1-912453-80-1 (hardback)
ISBN 978-1-912453-62-7 (paperback)
ISBN 978-1-912453-68-9 (e-book)

Printed and bound by CPI Group (UK) Ltd, Croydon, CRO 4YY

Notice
The information in this book is designed to orientate readers of the work under analysis,
to elucidate and contextualise its key ideas and themes, and to aid in the development
of critical thinking skills. It is not meant to be used, nor should it be used, as a
substitute for original thinking or in place of original writing or research. References and
notes are provided for informational purposes and their presence does not constitute
endorsement of the information or opinions therein. This book is presented solely for
educational purposes. It is sold on the understanding that the publisher is not engaged
to provide any scholarly advice. The publisher has made every effort to ensure that
this book is accurate and up-to-date, but makes no warranties or representations with
regard to the completeness or reliability of the information it contains. The information
and the opinions provided herein are not guaranteed or warranted to produce particular
results and may not be suitable for students of every ability. The publisher shall not be
liable for any loss, damage or disruption arising from any errors or omissions, or from
the use of this book, including, but not limited to, special, incidental, consequential or
other damages caused, or alleged to have been caused, directly or indirectly, by the
information contained within.

THE MACAT LIBRARY

The Macat Library is a series of unique academic explorations of seminal works in the humanities and social sciences – books and papers that have had a significant and widely recognised impact on their disciplines. It has been created to serve as much more than just a summary of what lies between the covers of a great book. It illuminates and explores the influences on, ideas of, and impact of that book. Our goal is to offer a learning resource that encourages critical thinking and fosters a better, deeper understanding of important ideas.

Each publication is divided into three Sections: Influences, Ideas, and Impact. Each Section has four Modules. These explore every important facet of the work, and the responses to it.

This Section-Module structure makes a Macat Library book easy to use, but it has another important feature. Because each Macat book is written to the same format, it is possible (and encouraged!) to cross-reference multiple Macat books along the same lines of inquiry or research. This allows the reader to open up interesting interdisciplinary pathways.

To further aid your reading, lists of glossary terms and people mentioned are included at the end of this book (these are indicated by an asterisk [*] throughout) – as well as a list of works cited.

Macat has worked with the University of Cambridge to identify the elements of critical thinking and understand the ways in which six different skills combine to enable effective thinking.
Three allow us to fully understand a problem; three more give us the tools to solve it. Together, these six skills make up the **PACIER** model of critical thinking. They are:

ANALYSIS – understanding how an argument is built
EVALUATION – exploring the strengths and weaknesses of an argument
INTERPRETATION – understanding issues of meaning

CREATIVE THINKING – coming up with new ideas and fresh connections
PROBLEM-SOLVING – producing strong solutions
REASONING – creating strong arguments

To find out more, visit **WWW.MACAT.COM.**

CONTENTS

CRITICAL THINKING AND *ON RELIGION*

Primary critical thinking skill: CREATIVE THINKING
Secondary critical thinking skill: INTERPRETATION

Friedrich Schleiermacher's 1799 text *On Religion* is an excellent illustration of the creative thinking process. In a series of five skillfully crafted speeches, Schleiermacher seeks to persuade a group of thinkers skeptical about organized religion and its social and political consequences that religion is an essential element of human life, which inevitably manifests itself in historical institutions patterned by specific rituals and beliefs. In doing so, Schleiermacher not only gathers together arguments ancient and contemporary to defend the centrality of religion to modern life, he also redefines religion as rooted in intuition and feeling. This is a definition that would come to have signal importance for Protestant Theology in the modern era.

Furthermore, Schleiermacher was a central figure in the emergence of the modern field of philosophical or "general" hermeneutics, which is the science of interpretation. *On Religion* is beautifully constructed and passionately argued. It reflects Schleiermacher's preoccupation with the nature of language. He believed that there is an essential connection between the cultural, national and ethnic identity of a particular group of people, and the way that group speaks, writes, and expresses itself through language.

ABOUT THE AUTHOR OF THE ORIGINAL WORK

Friedrich Schleiermacher was born in Breslau, Prussia, in 1768, and became not only one of Germany's most luminous intellects in the age of Kant, Schelling and Hegel, but also a pioneer of German nationalism. His first book, *On Religion*, was written while he was immersed in Early German Romanticism. It is a rhetorically brilliant exploration of the role religion should play in the modern world, which defines faith in terms of intuition and feeling. A passionate theological educator, Schleiermacher was dedicated throughout his later life to his vocation as an ordained minister in the Reformed Protestant church. He is now remembered as "The Father of Modern Protestant Theology."

ABOUT THE AUTHOR OF THE ANALYSIS

Dr Ruth Jackson did postgraduate work in theology and religious studies at the University of Cambridge. She is currently a Research Fellow in theology at Sidney Sussex College, Cambridge. Previously, she was a postdoctoral researcher at the Centre for Research in the Arts, Social Sciences and Humanities in Cambridge, where she worked on the ERC-funded project "The Bible and Antiquity in Nineteenth-Century Culture."

ABOUT MACAT

GREAT WORKS FOR CRITICAL THINKING

Macat is focused on making the ideas of the world's great thinkers accessible and comprehensible to everybody, everywhere, in ways that promote the development of enhanced critical thinking skills.

It works with leading academics from the world's top universities to produce new analyses that focus on the ideas and the impact of the most influential works ever written across a wide variety of academic disciplines. Each of the works that sit at the heart of its growing library is an enduring example of great thinking. But by setting them in context – and looking at the influences that shaped their authors, as well as the responses they provoked – Macat encourages readers to look at these classics and game-changers with fresh eyes. Readers learn to think, engage and challenge their ideas, rather than simply accepting them.

WAYS IN TO THE TEXT

KEY POINTS

- Friedrich Schleiermacher was a nineteenth-century theologian who is often referred to as the "Father of Modern Protestant* Theology."

- *On Religion* defends the value of religion in the Age of Enlightenment,* and defines its essence as feeling and intuition.

- The text is distinctive for the insight it gives into Early German Romanticism* and its characterization of Enlightenment thought.

Who was Friedrich Schleiermacher?

Friedrich Schleiermacher (1768–1834) was born in Breslau, Prussia.* He spent his childhood at a boarding school run by the Moravian Brethren,* a Protestant church community who placed an emphasis on personal faith and preaching and teaching the gospel. Although Schleiermacher would later speak fondly of the Moravian community, he left in his late teens after professing religious doubts, and joined the University of Halle* as a theology student.

Schleiermacher overcame his doubts, reasserted his Christian faith and, after leaving university, he passed his theological examinations to become a Reformed Church minister. Following a tutoring job in East Prussia, he moved to Berlin in his late twenties. While he was

chaplain of a hospital in the city, he became a celebrated member of Berlin's intellectual salon* culture and immersed himself in early German Romanticism. He published *On Religion* at this time, his most significant and contentious text in the field of philosophy of religion, and one that would establish his reputation throughout the German-speaking world.

Schleiermacher proceeded to hold professorships first at Halle and then the newly founded University of Berlin. He had a field-changing influence within theology, hermeneutics* and ethics. He also became a prominent public figure in later life. He was a key voice for early German nationalism* during the upheavals of the Napoleonic Wars,* and supported the unification of the Lutheran* and Reformed* divisions of German Protestantism before the Prussian Union of Churches* in 1817.

Schleiermacher's thought stands as a monument to the tension between Enlightenment rationalism* and German Romantic philosophy, and has had a tremendous influence on the history of modern Protestant thought. His irreverent portrait of Christianity in *On Religion* and his association with the Romantics made his contemporaries in the German Reformed Church wary of this influence. In the twentieth century, Protestant theologian Karl Barth* condemned his theology as liberal.* Barth also critiqued Schleiermacher's use and defense of the category "religion," as a general category. Today, Schleiermacher continues to divide opinion within theological circles, both harshly criticized and well respected.

What does *On Religion* say?

In *On Religion*, Schleiermacher argues that religion is a vital and universal aspect of human life, and seeks to defend it from modern, historical and scientific forms of criticism. He denies that it is fundamentally about morality, ritual, scripture or dogma. He argues that these features, while integral to the way religion is expressed and

practiced in the world, are only secondary. Instead, the essence of religion for Schleiermacher is intuition and feeling. This is so because the fundamental relationship religion refers to—the relation between the finite and the Infinite—is not one that can be conceived or represented in human thought.

By portraying religion's core as one of feeling, Schleiermacher sought to rescue its reputation in the eyes of its "cultured despisers", among whom he counted his Romantic friends, like Friedrich Schlegel* and Novalis.* He argues that many of the aspects these critics find unappealing about established religion are down to its being corrupted by culture, society and the meddling state. He asserts that there are numerous legitimate forms of religion in the world, each one of them a particular intuition of the Infinite in the finite. Most controversially for his Christian colleagues, Schleiermacher even contends that the notion of "God" is not essential to religion.

Schleiermacher is adamant, however, that although religion's essence is intuition and feeling, it cannot exist in the world in a pure form, separate from thought, language, rationality and human action. Nor is religion *irrational*. In his view, reason and feeling are both parts of the greater whole of human life. Schleiermacher's final two speeches accordingly make the point that religion is inherently social, and that religion always exists in the world in a "positive" form, like Judaism, Hinduism or Islam. But Schleiermacher also contends that religion, conceived positively like this, does not stifle creativity and individuality as its critics may fear, with restrictive dogmas and moral strictures. Indeed, for Schleiermacher, religion actually provides the human community and shared vision of life that uniquely allow individuals to flourish.

In his introduction to a special centenary edition of *On Religion*, the theologian Rudolf Otto* described it as "one of the most famous books that history has recorded and preserved."[1] Today, well

over two hundred years on from its original publication, the text retains its importance in Schleiermacher's native Germany as a foundational work in theology and religious studies. It is also a classic work of German literature more generally. Resplendent with allusions to ancient literature, mythology, art and poetry, as well as to the natural world, it testifies to the urgency with which Schleiermacher, as a Romantic, sought to challenge the moralism and rationalism of Enlightenment culture. It reflects the Romantic purpose of encouraging personal expression, and inspiring in the German language a new literary tradition worthy of the ancients.

Schleiermacher published three editions of the text over the course of his career. The original 1799 edition was written principally for a small audience of friends, Romantics, and other "cultured despisers" of religion. Schleiermacher's later editions, published in 1806 and 1821 respectively, were edited to address the concerns of a much wider audience, and to match the developments in his thought since 1799. Schleiermacher worked hard to explain passages that he thought had been misunderstood, and to bring the shape of the argument into line with conventional academic standards.

Why does *On Religion* matter?

In *On Religion*, Schleiermacher works to provide a compelling definition of religion, an attempt to save it from being misunderstood and rejected by his contemporaries. This definition would go on to have seminal importance not only for the Christian tradition, but also for the university disciplines of religious studies and comparative religion. But Schleiermacher's task was not merely academic or intellectual. He designed these speeches to challenge the outlook, basic convictions, and even the way of life of its audience. The text was urgently and passionately written, as well as systematically organized, with each speech building on the conclusion of the last. Schleiermacher

is a master of his material and his ideas. He delivers them in a direct and imaginative way, drawing on personal experience as well as literary motifs and imagery that he knows will endear him to his readers. The work is a brilliant historical example of persuasive writing and testifies to Schleiermacher's skills in rhetoric and oratory.

On Religion also gives a student in the twenty-first century an insight into Schleiermacher's exciting intellectual, cultural, and social world. We learn about the chief concerns of the Romantics, and their disdain for the established Christian church, with its hierarchy, priests, and entanglements with the state. We learn about Schleiermacher's characterization of Enlightenment rationalism, and his conviction that "prudent and practical people" are the death of religion—not doubters, scoffers, or immoral people, as the reader might have expected.[2]

A distinctive facet of *On Religion* is the way that its free and expressive style reflects Schleiermacher's convictions about both human nature and the nature of religion. Firstly, he stresses, for example, throughout the work that true religion cannot be taught, or forced on a person from outside. Religion concerns the inner life of feeling, and so people must become religious for themselves. The text therefore aims to be inspirational and encouraging, rather than dogmatic, matching Schleiermacher's commitment to human development and free expression.

Secondly, however, Schleiermacher is also adamant that religion by its very essence cannot be fully grasped or explained. Our words fail us, when we try to speak or write about the meaning of religion and the goal of the religious life. So while the text defines religion, it also gestures openly towards eventual mystery—"religion is sensibility and taste for the infinite"; "religion is intuition and feeling"—instead of pinning it down to a formula or concrete teaching.

NOTES

1   Rudolf Otto, "Introduction," in *On Religion: Speeches to Its Cultured Despisers,* trans. John Oman (New York: Harper and Row, 1958), ·•

2   Friedrich Schleiermacher, *On Religion: Speeches to its Cultured Despisers*, translated by Richard Crouter (Cambridge: Cambridge University Press, 1988), 59.

SECTION 1
INFLUENCES

MODULE 1
THE AUTHOR AND THE
HISTORICAL CONTEXT

KEY POINTS

- *On Religion* is a striking defense of religion's value in the modern world.

- Friedrich Schleiermacher was brought up in a devoutly Christian household. He suffered but later overcame a crisis of faith in his youth.

- Schleiermacher rose to prominence in Prussia in the aftermath of the French Revolution.*

Why Read This Text?

On Religion was written in Berlin in 1799. At a time when religious belief was waning among the educated classes of modern Europe, Schleiermacher argues passionately and systematically that religion is a universal and vital element of human life. He seeks to defend it from criticisms issuing from contemporary scientific, historical, and moral thought, and in doing so denies that the essence of religion is any series of practices, teachings or moral ideas. Instead, he defines the heart of religion as intuition and feeling.

The text is beautifully written, and is still enjoyed today in Schleiermacher's native Germany as a classic of modern literature. It offers a remarkable insight into the intellectual climate of late eighteenth-century Prussia, including the author's rejection of Immanuel Kant's* moral thought, his respect for the philosophy of Baruch Spinoza,* his perspective on Enlightenment rationalism, and his involvement in the Early German Romantic circle.

> **❝** No matter what one's attitude toward Schleiermacher's method and his utterances on religion may be, one is time and again enthralled by his original and daring attempt to lead an age weary with and alien to religion back to its very mainsprings; and to re-weave religion, threatened with oblivion, into the incomparably rich fabric of the burgeoning intellectual life of modern times. **❞**
>
> Rudolf Otto, Introduction to Friedrich Schleiermacher's *On Religion: Speeches to Its Cultured Despisers*

The book is also of historical importance as a central text in the founding and development of religious studies and comparative religion as academic disciplines. Schleiermacher's attempt to use "religion" as a universal category which can be validly applied across different "religious" traditions has been criticized by some scholars who find this universal application reductive and misleading. Links have been drawn between Schleiermacher's conception of religion, and an emerging colonial consciousness in the nineteenth century, which used the category of religion to describe colonized populations.[1]

The text continues to be studied widely and deeply appreciated by students in both Europe and the United States.

Author's Life
Friedrich Schleiermacher was born in 1768, in Breslau, Prussia. He was the eldest of three children, and came from a line of Reformed Church ministers on his mother's side. His father was a Reformed chaplain in the Prussian army. When Schleiermacher was a young boy, his father came into contact with a community of Moravian Brethren, and was profoundly impressed by their piety. The three children were sent to be educated in the community.

Schleiermacher would leave his Moravian school in 1787, citing a crisis of faith and disagreements with central points of Christian doctrine, including the divinity of Jesus Christ.[2] Nevertheless, his time with the Moravian Brethren made a deep impression upon his religious sensibility, and later, in 1802, he claimed that it was here that he "first developed that mystical disposition which is so essential to me and has saved and preserved me under all the assaults of skepticism."[3] Schleiermacher continued his education at the University of Halle, a liberal institution in Germany which, in deep contrast to his Moravian upbringing, was infused with the academic rationalism of Gottfried Wilhelm Leibniz* and Christian Wolff.* It was here that he developed a fascination with the critical and moral philosophy of Immanuel Kant, and delighted in reading the ancient philosophy of Plato* and Aristotle.*

After leaving Halle, Schleiermacher took the theological exams that would prepare him to become a minister in the Prussian Reformed Church. He had overcome his crisis of faith. Following a period as a tutor for a family in East Prussia, Schleiermacher moved to Berlin in his late twenties, to take up a post as chaplain in a major hospital there, called the Charité. It was in this vibrant city that he met his close friend Friedrich Schlegel, and joined the celebrated literary salon founded and run by Henriette Herz.* It was at this point that he wrote *On Religion*. At the time when he was virtually unknown as an author and he published the book anonymously.

Author's Background

Schleiermacher wrote *On Religion* a decade after the Storming of the Bastille* took place. Although the political situation in Germany was comparatively peaceful, after the French Revolution, the Prussian authorities were anxious about social unrest. The Revolution did indeed provide intellectual stimulation for Schleiermacher's young Romantic friends in Berlin, in terms of what it implied about the

nature of social and political freedom. Yet their relationship to it was complex. In broad terms, their initial enthusiasm gave way to a more nuanced critical view, as the revolutionaries adopted, then privileged, rationalist Enlightenment principles.

It is worth noting that between 1788–97, there was a Prussian edict ensuring that all religious documents, teaching, and acts of public worship conformed with the established confession of the Prussian Church. Such censorship—the repression of academic freedom when it came to the study of religion—demonstrates the conservative religious background against which Schleiermacher was writing. His decision to publish the text anonymously, however, was typical of the period.

Around the time he published *On Religion*, Schleiermacher was engaged in two other writing projects which reveal significant socio-political views and interests. The first was his plan—later abandoned—to translate a travel diary written by the English writer David Collins. This diary detailed plans for a penal colony that the British government sought to establish in "New South Wales" (modern-day Australia). In Schleiermacher's day, German-speaking territories including Prussia did not have a colonial empire or program of colonial expansion to rival that of Britain and France. Yet, Schleiermacher's interest in this British colonizing project, and his notes on the indigenous people of New South Wales, gives us an insight into his social ideas. His understanding of the nature of "religion" includes a rudimentary consideration of non-Western culture and practice, which he compared unfavorably and disparagingly with what he considered the more "highly developed" cultural and religious life of his contemporaries in Europe.

The second writing project was Schleiermacher's intervention in a public discussion concerning legal parity between Christians and Jews in Berlin. In particular, he challenged the proposal that baptism and conversion to Protestant Christianity should be required for Jews

seeking political emancipation and German citizenship. Jews in the city were not yet afforded civil rights,* but Schleiermacher protested that these should be offered to all Germans, regardless of religion.

NOTES

1   See Kwok Pui-lan, *Postcolonial Imagination and Feminist Theology* (Louisville, KY: Westminter/John Knox Press, 2005).

2   See the account in B. A. Gerrish, *A Prince of the Church: Schleiermacher and the Beginnings of Modern Theology* (Philadelphia: Fortress Press, 1984), 25.

3   Letter from April 5, 1783, in *Aus Schleiermacher's Leben in Briefen,* ed. Ludwig Jonas and Wilhelm Dilthey, 4 vols., 2nd ed. (Berlin: Reimer, 1860-1863), Volume 1, 294.

MODULE 2
ACADEMIC CONTEXT

KEY POINTS

- At the end of the eighteenth century, Protestant theology in Germany was being challenged by developments in the natural sciences.

- The role of reason in theological enquiry was conceived differently by two influential theological traditions— Pietism* and Neology.*

- The primary academic influences on *On Religion* were Schleiermacher's Romantic friends and interlocutors.

The Work in its Context

In Germany at the turn of the eighteenth to the nineteenth century— as was the case in Europe more widely—one of the greatest challenges facing Protestant theology was the increasing tension perceived between Christian faith on the one hand and the progress made in the natural sciences on the other. As natural scientists grew more adept at measuring the physical world and understanding its causal patterns, claims made by the Christian church about the creation of the world, the nature of the creator God, the existence of miracles and the divinity of Jesus Christ came under a heightened degree of intellectual scrutiny. None of these "supernatural" claims could be measured or tested with scientific instruments, and scientific voices were becoming more authoritative.

Protestant thinkers and theologians were also challenged at this time by the development and application of historical criticism.* This is a method of reading a text which seeks to understand it in terms of its original context, and also involves researching the original author(s),

> 66 If you put yourselves on the highest standpoint of metaphysics and morals, you will find that both have the same object as religion, namely, the universe and the relationship of humanity to it. This similarity has long been a basis of manifold aberrations; metaphysics and morals have therefore invaded religion on many occasions... 99
>
> Friedrich Schleiermacher, *On Religion: Speeches to Its Cultured Despisers*

their purposes, and the intended audience. Reading the Bible according to this method, and treating it like any other historical work, called its authority into question while also questioning Christian beliefs about the truth of the text and its nature as divinely inspired.

Meanwhile, in contrast, the Protestant theologian and literary critic Johann Gottfried Herder* (1744–1803) advocated a way of reading the Bible—and especially the Old Testament*—that focused on questions of aesthetics,* and paying attention to the text's poetic, literary quality. As was the case in the historical-critical approach, Herder stated that the interpreter should not approach the text with religious assumptions, beliefs, or a theological agenda. The Bible, in other words, should be treated as a collection of human documents, which have been written by people in particular places at particular times. Schleiermacher too would proceed to hold this view—that the Bible should be read like any other text.

Overview of the Field

In the second half of the eighteenth century, a way of thinking called "Neology" emerged within German theology. It stressed that religious truth—including proof for the existence of God—could be found through rational enquiry. The Neologians sought to highlight the consonance between revealed Christian teachings and natural human

reason. Their aim was to study the Bible from a rigorously historical and scientific perspective, as free as possible from preconceived ideas about its meaning. They also held the central aspects of Christian faith to be its moral teachings.

In sharp contrast, the Pietist tradition that had become widespread in Germany by the mid-eighteenth century, influencing both Lutheran and Reformed Church communities, was characterized by its emphasis on personal piety and inner, spiritual transformation. Pietists did not approach the Bible from a historical-critical angle or consider human reason to be the prime criterion for determining the value of this divinely-inspired text. Bible study was for them a necessary act of devotion; they expected their lives and wills to be formed by attention to the holy scriptures.

These two disparate movements influenced and structured theological discourse at the time that Schleiermacher was studying at the University of Halle.[1] However, there was also a third significant perspective on this issue of what role reason plays in theological enquiry, and this was the critical philosophy of Immanuel Kant.

Kant challenged contemporary rationalist accounts of the concept of God as the fundamental "constitutive" principle, one that grounds and explains the order of the world. Indeed, in Kant's view, questions about the existence of God or the origin of the universe were beyond the limit of rational enquiry, and could not be proved or disproved through reason. Instead, Kant proposed that the concept of God, when considered correctly, functions as a "regulative" principle in causal accounts of the order of the world. This means that the concept of God can *guide* empirical enquiry, but it cannot be given or realized in human experience.

Academic Influences

Schleiermacher began his education among the Moravian Brethren, whose theology was heavily influenced by Lutheran Pietism. At the

University of Halle, he was taught by rationalist theologians and encountered the work of the Neologian Johann S. Semler.* Schleiermacher also studied Kant's philosophy in depth at this time, and there is general agreement that he was profoundly influenced by Kant's moral philosophy in particular.

Schleiermacher accepted Kant's position that the moral law is the pronouncement of reason, and that to live in accord with reason is the highest good. After leaving Halle, however, Schleiermacher then wrote a series of essays critiquing Kant's understanding of human freedom, which he thought gave a falsely dualistic picture of human identity and action. In *On Religion*, we also see how he became profoundly critical of Kant's decision to conceive and define religion in terms of its relationship to morality. Nevertheless, when it came to religion and the realm of theology, Schleiermacher always respected the limits that Kant put on rational enquiry. He agreed that God's existence could not be "proved" through reason.

Further theological and philosophical influences on Schleiermacher, from his time at Halle through to his arrival in Berlin in 1796, include the seventeenth-century philosopher Baruch Spinoza, and contemporary thinkers Herder and Friedrich Heinrich Jacobi.* Once in Berlin, however, and established in the Romantic circle of Friedrich Schlegel, Novalis, and Ludwig Tieck,* Schleiermacher found himself in an intimate intellectual community that—united not least in their love of Platonic philosophy and ancient Greek art and poetry—encouraged and influenced each other in their ideas, their reading, and their writing projects.

One such writing project was the *Athenaeum Journal*, edited by the Schlegel brothers, and running to six issues from 1798 to 1800. This literary magazine, the founding publication of German Romanticism, contained poetry, fragments and philosophical tracts. But Schleiermacher and Schlegel also embarked on a joint project to

translate all of Plato's dialogues into German, and to introduce these dialogues in a critical edition available to the German public.

NOTES

1   See Kevin Vander Schel, *Embedded Grace: Christ, History, and the Reign of God in Schleiermacher's Dogmatics*, (Philadelphia: Fortress Press, 2013).

MODULE 3
THE PROBLEM

KEY POINTS

- A chief topic of debate for the German Romantics was the issue of human fulfilment, which they linked closely with freedom.

- Unlike Schleiermacher, the German Romantics were willing to speak of a "religion of art" and to unite art and religion in the quest for self-realization.

- Schleiermacher, a minister in the Prussian Reformed Church, disagreed with the Romantics about the value of organized religion.

Core Question

The key concern that was live among the Romantics, and provided the broader context for Schleiermacher's discussions with them about the nature and purpose of religion, was the issue of human flourishing or fulfilment, and how this is to be achieved.

For all of the Romantics, including Schleiermacher, human self-fulfillment went hand in hand with freedom. Instead of conceiving freedom as a negative concept—the absence of bonds or pressures—they saw it as a positive and constructive task. Freedom meant a process of self-disclosure or self-expression. As one scholar puts it: "The Romantics' fundamental ethical ideal was *Bildung*,* self-realization, the development of all human and individual powers into a whole."[1] In his poem "Das Athenaeum", Friedrich Schlegel suggested that it is *Bildung*, or self-development, which brings unique individuals into faithful community with one another.

> **❝** Especially now, the life of cultivated persons is removed from everything that would in the last way resemble religion. . . You have succeeded in making your earthly lives so rich and many-sided that you no longer need the eternal, and after having created a universe for yourselves, you are spared from thinking of that which created you. **❞**
>
> Friedrich Schleiermacher, *On Religion: Speeches to Its Cultured Despisers*

In other words, the Romantics did not see personal freedom and personal expression as being at odds with the good of society as a whole. Instead, the task of individual *Bildung* was a part of this good, and it was also a political activity. Indeed, the Romantics charged themselves with liberating "the spirit from all forms of social and political oppression."[2] This meant highlighting and confronting those institutional structures, values, and social norms that they believed prevented certain individuals from flourishing in contemporary Prussian society.

The Participants

A significant forerunner to the Romantics in their conception of *Bildung*, or self-realization, was the philosopher Johann Gottfried Herder. Across his work, including his essay "Another Philosophy of History for the Education of Mankind," Herder's view is that the cultural development of the individual takes place in relation to the greater society.

Another strand to this debate is that Schleiermacher and his Romantic contemporaries all saw art and aesthetics* as fundamental modes of self-expression. Some of the Romantics were prepared to go even further and, unlike Schleiermacher, sought to synthesize art and religion. Indeed, although Schleiermacher considered them in many

ways to be "cultured despisers" of religion, far from *rejecting* the idea of religion altogether, the Romantics aimed to bring it into line with their own expressive and aesthetic purposes. Friedrich Schlegel spoke of a "religion of art," and had ambitions to launch a new mythology and provide the increasingly scientifically-minded and secular Germany with a new shared source of meaning.

Schleiermacher himself believed that artistic genius could provoke religious responses, and could also acknowledge the value of an "artistic religion," such as the Ancient Greeks enjoyed with their poetic mythology. This much is evident in *On Religion*. However, he did not agree with Schlegel that art could be the essence of religion.

The Contemporary Debate

Texts which tell us about the broader Romantic perspective on religion at this time include Friedrich Schlegel's "Ideas" (1800), and Novalis's essay "Christendom or Europe" (1799). These works indicate that the key difference between Schleiermacher and the other Romantics centers on the latter's distrust of what we could call organized religion, including Schleiermacher's own Protestant Christianity. Such distrust was nothing new among elite Prussian intellectuals, artists, and musicians. Before Novalis and Schlegel, Friedrich Schiller* and Johann Wolfgang von Goethe,* who represent Weimar Classicism* were public critics and commentators on the established Church.

What sort of "religion," then, were the Romantics convinced by? To use the words of one commentator, they conceived religion as a rising beyond the push and pull of chaotic worldly life, and seeking a holy unity above it: "Novalis, and then Schlegel caught sight of a vision that dissolves time, transporting the visionary to a plane above change and temporality."[3]

In contrast, Schleiermacher was convinced throughout his life that religion means seeking the Infinite *through* the finite realm. He was

adamant that humans, even spiritually, cannot escape the boundaries of space and time in this life. In his view, the world's historical religious traditions—including their priests, rituals, special buildings and places—embraced this fact. These traditions, the "determinate forms of religion," were for him the only way in which religion exists and can be practiced in the world, among "finite and limited beings."[4] He spends the fifth speech of *On Religion* defending them in this manner.

Meanwhile, in a telling philosophical fragment written about this time, Schlegel denies the "need" for a mediating Christ figure, through whom finite humans are put into touch with the Infinite. For Schlegel, all creative individuals are capable of mediating the divine. He writes: "It's only prejudice and presumption that maintains there is only a single mediator between God and man. For the perfect Christian . . . everything would really have to be a mediator."[5]

NOTES

1   Frederick Beiser, *The Romantic Imperative* (Cambridge, MA: Harvard University Press, 2003), 25.

2   Beiser, *Romantic Imperative*, 100.

3   Jack Forstman, A Romantic Triangle: Schleiermacher and Early German Romanticism, (Missoula, MT: Scholars Press, 1977) 116.

4   Friedrich Schleiermacher, *On Religion: Speeches to its Cultured Despisers*, translated by Richard Crouter (Cambridge: Cambridge University Press) 99.

5   Fragment 243, in Friedrich Schlegel, *Friedrich Schlegel's Lucinde and the Fragments,* trans. by Peter Firchow (Minneapolis: University of Minnesota Press, 1971) 194.

MODULE 4
THE AUTHOR'S CONTRIBUTION

KEY POINTS

- For Schleiermacher, the study of religion begins with the human subject, who is intuitively oriented towards the Infinite.

- *On Religion* doesn't fit conventional academic methodological boundaries, but it is a systematically argued and compelling text.

- Schleiermacher's own religious perspective cut against contemporary cultural attitudes to religion.

Author's Aims

The scholar Richard Crouter calls *On Religion* the "premier expression of an understanding of religion as rooted in immediate pre-reflexive feeling and intuition."[1] Schleiermacher was not the first theologian or philosopher to indicate that the study of religion could or should begin with the human subject, or that "the structures and workings of human subjectivity could be looked to for evidence of the divine."[2]

The reason, however, that Schleiermacher's religious thought is held to be distinctive and subtly original, and why he is often identified as someone who redefined religion for modernity, is that he combined this methodological turn towards the subject, with the understanding that humans are essentially and intuitively oriented towards the Infinite (or "the Universe," another word he uses in *On Religion*). In his mature work, *Christian Faith* (first edition 1821-22) Schleiermacher spoke of religious faith in terms of a "feeling of absolute dependence" upon the *Whence* of all finite existence.[3] It was in such terms that he understood religion to be a universal and essential element of life.

> ❝ I speak to you as a human being about the holy
> mysteries of humanity according to my view; about which
> was in me when, still with youthful enthusiasm, I sought
> the unknown; about that which has been the innermost
> mainspring of my existence ever since I have thought and
> been alive and which shall eternally remain for me the
> highest ... ❞
>
> Friedrich Schleiermacher, *On Religion: Speeches to Its Cultured Despisers*

In *On Religion*, Schleiermacher is not primarily interested in suggesting *what* his readers should believe. It is not a dogmatic text, and at no point does Schleiermacher reveal his status as a member of the Protestant clergy and it is only in his fifth speech, entitled "On the Religions," that Schleiermacher begins to discuss the significance of belonging to a particular religious tradition. He writes simply as a religious believer, aiming to persuade his readers to recognize their own innate, unique, and individual religiosities.

Approach

Schleiermacher composed the original edition of *On Religion* with great excitement and in less than half a year. The speed of the book's creation matches the urgency of both its style and its function. As Rudolph Otto comments, Schleiermacher sought to "re-weave religion, threatened with oblivion, into the incomparably rich fabric of the burgeoning intellectual life of modern times."[4] *On Religion* is also evidently a text that transgresses typical academic methodological boundaries, as these are understood nowadays. Schleiermacher's discussion of the nature of religion mounts a philosophical, ethical but primarily spiritual inquiry of the type: "what is the meaning of my life?" or "how should I perceive my relationships to the world, to other people and to God?"

Although the text has this clear spiritual end, however, this does not mean it lacks systematic argument or rigor. It is a masterfully structured and rhetorically powerful piece, reflecting Schleiermacher's critical command of contemporary philosophical theory, from the Romantics' reception of Plato and Spinoza, to Kant and Fichte.* Schleiermacher also critiques the rationalism of contemporary German culture, and the tendency of its institutions towards larger-scale management schemes which he argued were utilitarian* in nature, and detrimentally so.

In the original 1799 work—written when he was a relatively unknown author—Schleiermacher's strategy was to endear himself to his target audience of German intellectuals. He urges them that he understands their critiques of established or organized religion, realizes that religion is a tired and labored subject, but seeks to reassure them about its real and true essence. His style is playful and full of evocative imagery. He not only makes use of historical narratives and biblical texts, he also familiarly alludes to everyday, shared experience (another strategy to endear himself to his audience), plays upon cultural prejudices against the French and the English, and attacks the contemporary Protestant Church for its powerful financial and political position.

Contribution in Context

Schleiermacher's contribution to the modern understanding of religion was influenced by his education among the Moravian Brethren, his study of Spinoza, Plato, and Kant's critical philosophy, as well as his society with the German Romantics who were his confidants and companions. Nevertheless, it would be wrong to see Schleiermacher's ideas as simply received from other sources or shared with other thinkers. Rather, he developed a subtle and distinctive perspective on religion against the background of these divergent and often conflicting influences.

The distinctive quality of Schleiermacher's theological vision becomes clearer when it is juxtaposed with another religious perspective that developed in the late eighteenth and early nineteenth century, and became an influence on the Romantics themselves in their poetry and spiritual outlook. This is the consciousness of what Friedrich Schiller called a "godless nature"—a natural world divested of divine activity—in his 1788 poem "The Gods of Greece."[5]

In this poem, Schiller celebrates ancient Greek mythology for unifying divinity and nature, before mourning over the loss of such unity in modern culture. He laments that this beautiful divine world has receded over the horizon; the worldview now prevalent in Europe is a materialist one, which views the natural world in terms of a churning series of scientifically verifiable and observable causal processes. And in Schiller's mind, Protestant Christianity presents no real antidote to this worldview.

NOTES

1   Richard Crouter, 'Introduction,' in *On Religion: Speeches to its Cultured Despisers*, by Friedrich Schleiermacher (Cambridge: Cambridge University Press, 1988), ··.

2   Ben Quash, "Revelation," in *The Oxford Handbook of Systematic Theology*, eds. John Webster, Kathryn Tanner, and Iain Torrance (Oxford: Oxford University Press, 2007), 328-329.

3   Friedrich Schleiermacher, *Christian Faith*, translated by Terrence Tice, Catherine L. Kelsey, and Edwina Lawler, (Louisville, KY: Westminster John Knox Press, 2016), 24.

4   Rudolf Otto, 'Introduction,' in *On Religion: Speeches to Its Cultured Despisers*, by Friedrich Schleiermacher (New York, Harper and Row, 1958), ··.

5   Friedrich von Schiller, "Die Götter Griechenlands," Schillers Werke. Nationalausgabe, ed. Julius Petersen and Friedrich Beißner (Weimar 1943) Vol I, 190-195.

SECTION 2
IDEAS

MODULE 5
MAIN IDEAS

KEY POINTS

- In Schleiermacher's first three speeches, he deals with the essence of religion, and how religion relates to individual self-expression.

- Schleiermacher argues that religion is rooted in intuition.

- A scholar of hermeneutics and translation theory, Schleiermacher was interested in the nature of language and how it shapes self-expression.

Key Themes

On Religion comprises a succession of five speeches, each of which can be read as a separate and inwardly coherent chapter, though each in turn builds on the conclusion of the last. In this module, we will introduce the themes of Schleiermacher's first three speeches, leaving the topics of his final two addresses for the next module.

Schleiermacher's first speech, which he entitled "Apology", aims to convince his audience that he shares a fundamental perspective with them concerning the nature of reality and the self's relation to it. He explains that human souls are polarized (a common argument in eighteenth-century science and philosophy), that they are both active and passive, driven beyond themselves but also into themselves. Having enumerated this vision of life involving an "eternally continuous play of opposing forces" Schleiermacher proceeds to argue that such a view doesn't preclude living a religious life but, on the contrary, can form a fruitful basis for it.[1]

In his second speech, Schleiermacher turns to the essence of religion. He begins by implicitly drawing a distinction between

> **"** Praxis is an art, speculation is a science, religion is the
> sensibility and taste for the infinite. **"**
>
> Friedrich Schleiermacher, *On Religion: Speeches to Its Cultured Despisers*

himself and Kant. Religion is *not* morality, he stresses: "religion must
not use the universe in order to derive duties and is not permitted to
contain a code of laws."[2] Nor, Schleiermacher insists, is religion to
be confused with metaphysics. Indeed, he continues, "religion's
essence is neither thinking or acting, but intuition and feeling."[3] It is
such, because the object of religion—the Infinite, the highest
principle of reality—is not some "thing" that can be represented or
grasped in thought.

The Infinite is immediately present to the believer, but cannot be
known or processed or seen by the mind. The Infinite cannot be
proven or accessed through reason. It is in this light that Schleiermacher
tells his readers that "the highest and most universal formula of religion"
is "intuition of the universe." This formula is universal for him because
it is without dogmatic content. It does not assign any specific attributes
or properties to the Infinite but simply defines it as a kind of openness
to the transcendent. He can therefore happily include Spinoza's
pantheism* and ancient Greek religiosity within his remit.

In his third speech, Schleiermacher deals with the role of religion
in the self-cultivation (*Bildung*) of the individual. His central points
here are: all people are born with the capacity for religion; people
cannot be taught to intuit and one therefore cannot be "instructed" in
religion; religion develops in each person according to his or her
individual character unless their capacity for religion is "blocked."[4]

Exploring the Ideas

When Schleiermacher describes religion as rooted in "intuition,"
what does he mean? We have already seen that he distinguishes

intuition from reason, imagination, all thinking, language, and action, and that he places it before or beneath these human behaviors. So it may seem confusing when, elsewhere in the text, he likens the event of "intuiting" the Infinite to "sensing" and "tasting" it. What he is getting at here is that intuition is a primordial human state.

Religion lies behind, but is independent from all other human modes of being. He writes: "Intuition is and always remains something individual, set apart, the immediate perception, nothing more."[5] The religious sense in Schleiermacher's view thus doesn't *compete* with human activities or thoughts or views precisely because it is independent from them. This is important. Thinking, acting and doing do not grind to a halt you recognize that you, as a finite individual, exist in relation to the Infinite. Religious intuition is a background state. It is an accompaniment to life.

Another important point here is that Schleiermacher envisages intuition as a kind of *response* on the part of the human being. He writes: "All intuition proceeds from an influence of the intuited on the one who intuits, from an original and independent action of the former, which is then grasped, apprehended, and conceived by the latter according to one's own nature."[6] What gives rise to a religious intuition in the individual human being is the Universe, or the Infinite, or the Absolute (Schleiermacher uses these terms interchangeably) revealing itself to that person.

Religious intuitions are not produced by the inner workings of the human mind, or provoked by other people, the world, or any given object in it. Each and every one of these things is finite, unable to ground itself or generate itself, or indeed to ground or wholly sustain anything else. Instead, they exist in constant flux and change. By contrast, religious feeling responds to that which is whole, perfect, Infinite—and it transcends the finite order. Here then, we return to our previous point that for Schleiermacher, the Infinite is not something that can be represented or grasped in thought.

Language and Expression

For Schleiermacher—who in his later career would go on to make a foundational contribution to the modern field of hermeneutics, and was also a gifted translator—the theme of language itself was not an incidental consideration when it came to the process of writing. Like a number of his philosophical influences, including Plato and Herder, he was fascinated by language and how it enables human development, both individually and socially.

In his *Soliloquies*, a short book written in 1800, Schleiermacher contends that the language communities share keeps them together as an inwardly coherent group. Shared language, including its grammatical rules and patterns, shapes the individual members of a society as they grow up, equipping them with tools but also with boundaries for self-expression. "Language has exact symbols in fine abundance for everything thought and felt in the world's sense", Schleiermacher explains — "it is the clearest mirror of the times, a work of art revealing the current spirit."[7]

The way that Schleiermacher expresses himself in *On Religion* is particularly appropriate to his subject matter. It also picks up on his distinctive vision of people as rational "organs" of the universe—mouthpieces through which the universe communicates meaning, and even comes to know itself. In some dramatic lines at the beginning the book, Schleiermacher writes: "That I speak does not originate from a rational decision or from hope or fear, nor does it happen in accord with some final purpose or for some arbitrary or accidental reason. It is the inner, irresistible necessity of my nature; it is a divine calling; it is that which determines my place in the universe and makes me the being that I am."[8] Repeatedly in *On Religion,* Schleiermacher's writing reflects the Romantic concern with human self-development and expression as central to human flourishing.

NOTES

1 Schleiermacher, *On Religion*, 5.

2 Schleiermacher, *On Religion*, 20.

3 Schleiermacher, *On Religion*, 22.

4 Schleiermacher, *On Religion*, 57.

5 Schleiermacher, *On Religion*, 26.

6 Schleiermacher, *On Religion*, 24-25.

7 Horace Leyland Freiss, trans., *Friedrich Schleiermacher's Soliloquies* (Chicago: Open Court Pub. Co., 1926), 64.

8 Schleiermacher, *On Religion*, 5.

MODULE 6
SECONDARY IDEAS

KEY POINTS

- Schleiermacher's final two speeches in *On Religion* focus on the social element of religion, and on historical religious communities.

- *On Religion* has foundational importance for the academic disciplines of religious studies and comparative religion.

- Schleiermacher scholarship is interdisciplinary, and the text has been explored from numerous angles.

Other Themes

One could consider Schleiermacher's final two speeches as secondary ideas. These are: the social element of religion (in particular the institutions of the Church and the priesthood); and specific religious traditions themselves. Schleiermacher refers to these as the "positive" religions. These are secondary themes, insofar as Schleiermacher introduces them as developments of his primary points concerning the essence of religion as feeling, and his contention that the Infinite cannot be grasped, understood or defined by human minds.

However, to call these themes secondary does not render them any less significant to his overall argument. Indeed, without them— Schleiermacher urges that religion never exists in a pure state, but is always shared in historical communities—his argument is incomplete. "Each religion," Schleiermacher professes, "was one of the particular forms eternal and infinite religion *necessarily* had to assume among finite and limited beings."[1]

Schleiermacher begins his fourth speech by anticipating his audience's disdain both for religious social institutions and the priests

> ❝ Just as no human being can come into existence as an individual, without simultaneously, through the same act, also coming into a world, into a definite order of things, and being placed among individual objects, so also a religious person cannot attain his individuality without, through the same act, also dwelling in a determinate form of religion. ❞
>
> Friedrich Schleiermacher, *On Religion: Speeches to Its Cultured Despisers*

who lead and organize them. He suggests that people are suspicious of organized religion often because they imagine it to be stifling and constraining, made up of "lifeless mechanism and empty customs,"[2] Schleiermacher contends, however, that religion is *necessarily* social. He argues that it is human nature to express and communicate what we are most passionate about. With religion this is no different, and religious communities are founded and sustained, he thinks, by the continual reciprocation of religious intuitions and feelings among their members. As for priests, these are individuals who step forward to lead not to assert power or shut down creativity or life in religion. Rather, Schleiermacher defends them as people led by a "free stirring of the spirit," called to lead by example in communities that benefit from such inspiration and guidance.

In his fifth speech, Schleiermacher turns his attention to specific historical religious traditions. He begins by explaining that "no one can possess religion completely, for the human being is finite and religion is infinite. But ... religion is not able to be only partially parceled out among people, as much as each can grasp, but ... must organize itself in manifestations that are rather different from one another."[3] Given his contention that the Infinite cannot be grasped by human intellect, and his vision of the world as full of diversity and individuality—each nation and culture having its own language and

way of life—Schleiermacher defends the notion that there necessarily exists a plurality of religious traditions, each valid in its own unique way and stemming from a specific intuition of the Infinite in the finite.

His view is that religion cannot be discussed truly objectively. It can never appear as a merely "natural" object, knowable through reason, and always the same in every context. Rather, it must always take a "positive" form in the world, such that it is impossible to grasp its true meaning, except by a believer who has been "seized by the Universe" in a particular way.

Exploring the Ideas

As part of his defense of religion as a social phenomenon, Schleiermacher makes a distinction between what he describes as the true church—an eternal and incorruptible community of believers—and the church as it exists in the world. This is the *false* church, corrupted by the state, by society, and by its relationships with powerful organizations. In making this distinction between the true church and its "false" counterpart, Schleiermacher evokes the work of a long line of Christian theologians following the apostle Paul,* like Saint Augustine* and Martin Luther,* who conceived the worldly church as an imperfect institution which would find its fulfilment only at the end of time, when God's Infinite reality has fully penetrated that of the finite.

Schleiermacher's final chapter ends with a structural comparison of Christianity and Judaism. It was this practice of theorizing about the essence of religion in general, before contrasting different religious traditions, that has made Schleiermacher's text a foundational yet contentious one in the history of religious studies and comparative religion.

On the one hand, unlike many thinkers in the Christian tradition, Schleiermacher doesn't see a significant historical or doctrinal connection between Judaism and Christianity. Schleiermacher

regarded religions not as natural objects that can be wholly described and understood from the outside, but as traditions that only made sense to the believer. He wanted to declare Christianity and Judaism entirely separate communities. These religions have their own utterly unique practices, ideas, and texts—the Old Testament, he averred, is a Jewish and not a Christian document.

Nevertheless, for all the independence he sought to allot to various religious traditions, Schleiermacher paints an erroneous, derogatory and indeed harmful portrait of Judaism in *On Religion*. This reflects his practice of placing religious traditions in a fixed hierarchy, according to how perfectly religious he judges them to be. In the order he creates, he puts his own protestant Christianity first and fails to honor the particular characteristics of other faith traditions.

Overlooked

Schleiermacher remains an important figure in many academic disciplines so it would be both unwise and inaccurate to claim that *On Religion* is a neglected text, or that any of its major themes have been overlooked. As well as its obvious relevance in the fields of theology, religious studies and philosophy, scholars have also used it to investigate Schleiermacher's attitude toward politics, art, music, Classical literature, Enlightenment rationality and modern culture. It is also counted as a resource for students of intellectual history, many of whom are interested in Schleiermacher for his innovative contributions to early German nationalism though he never articulated a full, systematic nationalist agenda. However, he was one among a few prominent figures who saw a German nation-state as a potential solution to the political and social problems that German-speaking lands faced in the Napoleonic era.

On Religion has recently received a greater degree of critical scrutiny in the interests of discerning how and to what extent his theory of religion has had a negative impact on the academic treatment

of religions other than his own Christianity. Indeed, attention is rightly being drawn in particular to Schleiermacher's derogatory portrayal of Judaism in his fifth speech. Here, he declares that Judaism is a "dead" religion, implicating him in a wider problem of social and institutional anti-Judaism, at a time when Jewish people in Berlin did not enjoy full civil liberties, and Jewish scholars in Prussia were barred from teaching or taking up academic posts in universities.

NOTES

1   Schleiermacher, *On Religion*, 99.

2   Schleiermacher, *On Religion*, 72.

3   Schleiermacher, *On Religion*, 99.

MODULE 7
ACHIEVEMENT

KEY POINTS

- Schleiermacher's *On Religion* was knowingly provocative.

- At 29 years of age, Schleiermacher was encouraged to write the text by his close friends Henriette Herz and Friedrich Schlegel.

- Schleiermacher portrayed the Jewish religion in a negative and harmful way.

Assessing the Argument

Schleiermacher knew his presentation of religion as rooted in intuition and feeling was provocative and before publication he was anxious about the reaction of his peers and superiors in the Reformed church. He was not completely resigned to rejection and misunderstanding by theologians, however, and after his book was met with criticism, he kept this in mind and sought to address it in revised editions of the text in 1806 and then 1821.

Schleiermacher was a gifted preacher and cared about the art of communication, seeking to connect with his audience. So he was dismayed when his points were misconstrued. One of the major revisions he made in subsequent editions of the text was to modify his statement that "whether we have a God as a part of our intuition depends on the imagination."[1] This radical line was construed as flippant and heterodox by his fellow churchmen, who thought that Schleiermacher was rendering the God they believed in—the Trinitarian God—a product of the subjective human imagination. In the third edition of the text, Schleiermacher defends himself against these charges. He admits that this line about the human imagination

> **❝** Schleiermacher combined the far-reaching results of the Enlightenment, of Kant and our classical poetry, yet he stands alone in his deep reflectiveness in the inspired vision which was his; at the same time he turned these ideas towards a reform of the moral world and the development of the Christian religion; thus he turned men's minds towards the great tasks of the present. **❞**
>
> Wilhelm Dilthey, *Selected Writings*

was naive, but he stresses that he does not think God has an "impersonal" form, that is fleshed out by the human mind. He claims that his aim was to show instead that religious faith can take many forms. He goes on to compare himself to Saint Paul, who preached the gospel of Christ to the men of Athens and found they already had a certain type of piety. Schleiermacher also argues that it is not possible to "prove" or "deduce" through reason that God exists as a Trinity. The Trinity, he urges, can only be known through faith and in witness to the work of God in human history.

In addressing his friends the Romantics—the so-called "despisers" of religion—Schleiermacher aimed to persuade them of religion's value. It is striking then to find that almost ten years following the book's publication, Friedrich Schlegel and Ludwig Tieck had converted to Roman Catholicism. The timing is such that we cannot credit Schleiermacher with their conversion, especially since he was a great critic of Catholicism. The situation is nevertheless interesting.

Achievement in Context

The text is renowned today for reconciling the criticisms that the Enlightenment and German Romanticism respectively brought to traditional religion. It also acknowledges Kant's argument that the

existence of God cannot be proved through rational enquiry while showing an awareness of developments in the natural sciences. It stands as a testament to the status of religion at the turn of the nineteenth century, but its urgent restatement of *what religion is* was felt to be compelling and also necessary to many.

At the time of publication, the book won Schleiermacher a reputation among intellectuals in his homeland, where he had hitherto been an unknown and untested writer—simply a young hospital chaplain and preacher in Berlin. Within philosophical circles in particular, on its publication *On Religion* was immediately shared and read, although it was more warmly received and discussed among the intimate group of Romantic thinkers and writers to which Schleiermacher belonged, than it was among contemporary Idealists like Hegel,* Schiller, and Schelling.

In addition to his commitment to religious apologetics—his desire to defend the role of religion in the modern world—another external but rather personal pressure on Schleiermacher as he wrote the book was the encouragement of his close friends Schlegel and Henriette Herz. At their bidding, the 29-year-old, untested Schleiermacher completed his first published literary work, an essay for the Athenaeum journal, before embarking on the longer project of *On Religion*.[2]

Henriette Herz commented that, having read portions of the work in progress, she and Schlegel didn't seek to push Schleiermacher to change his arguments or positions where they disagreed with him. They wished the piece to come from him and testify to his own specific point of view. And yet, it is awash with Romantic imagery—Schleiermacher's style and his prioritizing of the theme of self-expression matches the nature of Schlegel's own concerns.

Limitations
On Religion came out of Schleiermacher's involvement with a specific Berlin intellectual set, immersed in the study of ancient art, philosophy,

and literature. For today's reader, therefore, the text contains a number of culturally pertinent references that may appear abstruse and require specialist knowledge to decipher. His reference to "the aged Simonides" at the start of his second speech, for instance, evokes a story from Cicero's* work *On the Nature of the Gods*. Similarly, spotting Schleiermacher's implicit critical references to Kant's philosophy as well as to various rationalist philosophical positions requires a trained eye. Richard Crouter's translation of the first edition highlights and provides notes on these moments.

Schleiermacher's text pushes open and confounds traditional academic boundaries. It does not meet the conditions to count as a modern work of religious studies since its argument (although systematically ordered) incorporates personal expression, experience, and opinion, and does not seek to study religion or compare religions from an objective or social-scientific perspective. It would be more appropriate to call *On Religion* a work of religious philosophy, demonstrating the author's gift for oratory, and with human flourishing as its core concern.

One aspect of Schleiermacher's text has been rightly denounced in the present day. This is his harmful portrayal of Judaism as a religion that was once beautiful and valuable, but is now, in the modern age, "dead." What he means by this claim is that Judaism has been corrupted, so that no spirit and no true religious quality is left in it—all that remains is a body of laws, texts and rituals. Schleiermacher's negative portrait of Judaism here reflected a broader trend of anti-Jewish thinking in early-nineteenth century Germany—a trend prevalent even among some of his own emancipated Jewish friends in Berlin.

As one scholar explains, following Moses' Mendelssohn's* example of "thorough acculturation" and what is now referred to as the "Jewish Enlightenment," a large section of Berlin's moneyed and well-educated Jewish community at this time "wished to shake off the

shackles of rigid religious tradition, and ensure the possibility of cultural and political life for themselves."[3] Schleiermacher's image of Judaism as "dead" fits in many ways with this desire, shared among his friends, to abandon specifically Jewish ceremonies, and to promote a "rational" Judaism instead, stripped of such practices.

In his book *Modern Religion, Modern Race*, Theodore Vial* has evaluated Schleiermacher's contribution (both negative and positive) to the development of the category of religion in modernity. A distinctively harmful aspect to Schleiermacher's legacy is this interpretation of the Jewish tradition.[4]

NOTES

1 Schleiermacher, *On Religion*, 53.

2 Friedrich Schleiermacher, *The Life of Schleiermacher: As Unfolded in His Autobiography and Letters*, ed. and trans. Frederica Rowan (London: Smith, Elder and Co., 1860), Vol 1., 139-140.

3 David Friedländer, Friedrich Schleiermacher and Wilhelm Abraham Teller, *A Debate on Jewish Emancipation and Christian Theology in Old Berlin*, eds. Richard Crouter and Julie Klassen (Indianapolis/Cambridge: Hackett Publishing Company, 2004) 9-10.

4 Theodore Vial, *Modern Religion, Modern Race* (Oxford: Oxford University Press, 2016).

MODULE 8
PLACE IN THE AUTHOR'S WORK

KEY POINTS

- Schleiermacher was preoccupied his whole life with the question of what it means to be religious.

- Schleiermacher's entire corpus can be profitably studied as an intellectually coherent whole.

- Although Schleiermacher's magnum opus was his later text, *Christian Faith*, *On Religion* was the one that made him famous.

Positioning

On Religion was Schleiermacher's first book-length published work. He was aged 30 at the time of its publication. Although it took less than six months to write, the understanding of religion he presents in the text is one he arrived at over the course of many years. Its roots lie in the pietistic theology of the Moravian Brethren, in whose community he grew up and went to school. As a means of charting Schleiermacher's intellectual development, it is striking to compare the mystical depth and spiritual aim of *On Religion* (1799), with the ethical scope of some of his earlier, youthful, and unpublished work. In *On the Highest Good* (1789), *On Human Freedom* (1790–3), and *On What Gives Value to Life* (1792–3), for instance, Schleiermacher critiques Kant's teaching about the transcendental freedom of the human self, and argues instead for a deterministic* account of human action. He was at this stage a university student at Halle (1787–90) before becoming a house tutor in East Prussia (1790–1793). Schleiermacher's academic interests at this point lay in expounding the nature of moral responsibility, the issue of human

> 66 When Schleiermacher, in his *Reden über die Religion*, preached the gospel of personal, immediate and emotional religion, he was only reasserting the Pietistic ideal, and continuing, in its religious phase, an individualistic movement of long duration. 99
>
> Walter Silz, *Early German Romanticism: Its Founders and Heinrich von Kleist*

freedom, the question of what it means to live a good life, and the causal relationships between the self and the world.

He was not yet writing explicitly or at length about what it means to be religious and indeed, prior to arriving at the University of Halle in 1787, Schleiermacher reported to his father that he was suffering a crisis of faith. He had begun to doubt central tenets of the Christian faith, including the very divinity of Christ, and at this point could not in all good conscience continue his theological education towards Christian ministry. However, through his study in particular of Kant, Spinoza, Plato and Aristotle, Schleiermacher equipped himself in this period with the technical vocabulary and philosophical apparatus that would later enable him to discuss religion from a philosophical as well as a theological and confessional angle.

The question of what it means to be religious, and how this affects ones thought and practices, is one that preoccupied Schleiermacher throughout his life.

Integration

Twenty years lie between the first edition of *On Religion* and Schleiermacher's greatest and most sophisticated theological work, the two-volume *Christian Faith*. The latter is the most famous text in modern Protestant theology. In it, Schleiermacher lists, describes, and interprets what he declares to be the essential doctrines of the

Protestant Christian Church. It was designed to give ministers in his own day a resource for teaching and preaching the faith.

Given the time distance between the two works and also the shift in Schleiermacher's professional status and intellectual priorities, it is commonplace for scholars to refer to "earlier Schleiermacher" and "later Schleiermacher." The former category indicates Schleiermacher's years among the Romantics in Berlin, his standing as a young Chaplain who wrote philosophical treatises in his spare time, and his interest in the motif of self-expression and self-cultivation. In addition to *On Religion*, his *Soliloquies*—an idealistic and quasi-autobiographical text that he completed in 1800—is characteristic of this period.

By contrast, Schleiermacher's "later period" began when he was a university preacher at Halle (1803–6), but usually indicates his time as professor of theology at the University of Berlin (1809–1834), where he also became president of the philosophy section of the Berlin Academy of the Sciences. While at Halle, Schleiermacher began to give versions of his famous lectures on hermeneutics and throughout his academic career he would also teach ethics, philosophy (dialectic), and theology.

Nevertheless, it is also possible and fruitful to study Schleiermacher's entire corpus as an intellectually coherent whole, in which there are important thematic and stylistic consistencies. In *On Religion*, Schleiermacher portrays piety as pre-reflective or non-cognitive. Not only does this prefigure his mature account of Christian faith as a "feeling of absolute dependence," but it also reflects his longstanding acceptance of Kant's teaching about the limitations of human reason before the ineffable nature of God.

Furthermore, Schleiermacher's conviction that religion is inherently communal has a prominent role both in the argument of *On Religion* and in the meaning of his later system of Christian Doctrine. The unity across Schleiermacher's corpus is evident, too, in

his consistent view that humans must seek the meaning of the Infinite through the finite. Arguably, this concept, which appears in *On Religion* in its most basic, abstract form manifests itself in Schleiermacher's mature theological work in his understanding that Jesus Christ is God made man: the Infinite literally made finite for humanity.

Significance

Not long after the publication of *On Religion* in 1799, the circle of Romantic thinkers and writers including Friedrich Schlegel and Henriette Herz, who had so shaped Schleiermacher's thought during the writing of his text, disbanded as a group and drifted apart. Schlegel and Schleiermacher fell out, and the former abandoned the Plato translation project they had agreed to do together, leaving Schleiermacher to complete it on his own.

This means scholars interested in analyzing Schleiermacher's corpus as a whole, or tracking the development of his thought, must consider whether Romanticism—the mode and style of thinking that dominates *On Religion*, with its critique of Kantian philosophy and its reinvigoration of ancient Greek mythology and poetry—was simply a passing phase. There is no scholarly consensus on the extent and nature of Schleiermacher's commitment to Romanticism. What can be said is that, although the text represents a very distinctive period in Schleiermacher's early life, it is one that he sought to bring with him into his later career, as he matured theologically and professionally, and became a professor of theology at the University of Berlin.

Schleiermacher's later work *Christian Faith*—in which Schleiermacher seeks to describe all teachings essential to the Protestant church, in their entirety—overshadows *On Religion* in terms of its magisterial size, its systematic presentation, the rigor of its scholarship and its engagement with previous systems of church

teaching. Although it was his first book, *On Religion* was the text that made Schleiermacher famous. It established his reputation as a masterfully innovative (albeit heterodox) Christian thinker and remains his most widely read work and a central, striking, and defining part of his legacy as a writer and thinker.

SECTION 3
IMPACT

MODULE 9
THE FIRST RESPONSES

KEY POINTS

- In theological circles, *On Religion* received sharp criticism on its release.

- In his responses to the criticisms of his mentor, F. S. G. Sack,* Schleiermacher defends and refines his theory of religion.

- *On Religion* was not translated into English until around a century after its original publication.

Criticism

Within traditional Christian theological circles, *On Religion* was initially eyed with suspicion. In contrast with the relative success he enjoyed among his philosopher friends and correspondents, he received little positive attention among his fellow ministers and preachers in the Reformed church. Schleiermacher had made reference to Spinoza in the text—a controversial figure among churchmen, rationalist theologians and Pietist minds alike, because of the pantheist* and materialist* qualities of his metaphysical system. Indeed, Spinoza was regarded as an atheist in Schleiermacher's day because of his argument that everything in the universe was determined by its relation to everything else, as the universe itself is a self-relating and self-generating whole.

Schleiermacher did not actually read Spinoza's work himself—he gained access to it only through the work of Friedrich Heinrich Jacobi. Nevertheless, this connection, together with his allusions throughout *On Religion* to the Infinite or Universe as the object of

> **❝** My dearest Schleiermacher! Had my heart hung less on you, had I not placed so much value upon the hope that you would have the strength and will to erect a sturdy dam against the stream of sophistry characteristic of our age, then it would not be so grievous to me that you have allowed yourself to be swept away by this very stream. **❞**
>
> A letter to Schleiermacher, in 1801, from Friedrich Samuel Gottfried Sack.

religion, and his contention that "whether we have a God as a part of our intuition depends on the imagination" repelled Schleiermacher's peers and superiors in the Reformed church.[1]

The charged personal letter that F. S. G. Sack, Schleiermacher's mentor, wrote to him about the text in 1801 is one example. Sack condemned the heterodox elements in *On Religion* and rebuked Schleiermacher for his close association with Friedrich Schlegel and the Romantics. Schlegel's 1800 novel *Confidential Letters on Lucinde*, modeled on his own relationship with Dorothea Veit,* had caused a great scandal and this reinforced Sack's low opinion of the group and their values. Indeed, although Sack did approve *On Religion* on behalf of the Prussian censorship board, he made it clear to Schleiermacher that he did not think the text was an object worthy of Christian study. Bitterly, he instead expressed his surprise that the author of such a text would insist on remaining a Christian minister and practicing preacher.

Among the Romantics whom Schleiermacher counted as the intended audience of his text—those "cultured despisers of religion," who were now gathered in the city of Jena—the text was received warmly and with much interest and energy. Novalis's work *Christendom or Europe* (1799) was directly inspired by it.

Responses

In his 1802 book *Faith and Knowledge*, G. W. F. Hegel described Protestantism thus: "[it] makes communion with God and consciousness of the divine into something inward that maintains its fixed form of inwardness; it makes them into a yearning for a beyond and a future."[2] Hegel proceeds to claim that this "protestant principle"—one of inwardness and individual "yearning"—reaches its "highest level" in Schleiermacher's portrayal of religion. Hegel's prominence as a philosopher alone makes this worthy of note, and here we find him highlighting *On Religion*, just a couple of years after its publication, as a particularly fine example of a specific religious mode of life and thought. Before this too, in 1801, Hegel had praised *On Religion*—respecting it as a text that recognized the contemporary need for a newly convincing understanding of religion.[3]

However, in later years, after the publication of Schleiermacher's *Christian Faith*, Hegel would develop a very critical view of the former's description of religion as "a feeling of absolute dependence." This much is clear from his quip that "a dog would be the best Christian for it possesses this in the highest degree, and lives mainly in this feeling."[4] Interestingly, however, Schleiermacher and Hegel never addressed each other in public dialogue, or directly reviewed or discussed each other's work in the public sphere. Schleiermacher's own responses to the critics of his text included his lengthy and defensive reply to F. S. G. Sack's letter. Here, Schleiermacher defends his vocation as a Christian preacher and in reply to Sack's concern that he represents God in an "impersonal" way, Schleiermacher stresses again that religion isn't generated out of any concept, or fixed idea, or projection of the human intellect. True religion is always a response of the finite mind to the Infinite, which cannot be grasped or held or analyzed in human thought and language. For Schleiermacher, indeed, "no religion evolves out of the concept of the personality of God."[5]

Conflict and Consensus

The relationship between Schleiermacher and his former mentor, Sack, was strained by this correspondence in 1801 and by the content of *On Religion*. It wasn't, however, severed and each retained a high regard for the other.[6]

Sack's disapproval of Schleiermacher's choice in friends, however, is indicative of a problem he faced more broadly in theological circles, concerning his personal reputation as a scholar, and what he and his work represented to traditional minds. Sack had denounced Schleiermacher's book as damagingly heterodox—as "nothing more than a spirited apology for pantheism, a rhetorical presentation of the Spinozic system."[7]

Overseas, too, in the English-speaking world in particular, Schleiermacher had a reputation negative enough to prevent his work from being readily translated or studied. Schleiermacher's hermeneutical theory, and the fact that he embraced historical criticism* as a way of reading and studying the Bible, also meant that he was viewed with suspicion. *On Religion* was not published in English until 1893—almost a century after it was originally written—when John Oman released a translation of its third edition. Moreover, such was the reputation Schleiermacher's name carried that, in 1825, J. C. Thirlwall, a fellow of Trinity College, Cambridge, was denied a promotion to Bishop in the Anglican* church due to concerns over his orthodoxy. Thirlwall had translated Schleiermacher's *Essay on the Gospel of Luke* into English, and this was cause for suspicion among the church authorities.[8]

Schleiermacher's decision to issue revised editions of *On Religion* over the course of his career suggests that he listened to his critics and their assessments of his work. In order to defend his theory of religion, but also to make some concessions to those who called him heterodox, he made substantial alterations to the text for two new issues in 1806 and 1821, and also added lengthy "explanations" to

each speech in 1821, explaining the reasoning behind his changes, together with a defense of his own theological position. Then, in 1831, a fourth edition came out with a few minor changes added. And yet, it is worth stressing that in his later career as a Professor of theology in Berlin, Schleiermacher never abandoned the work or denounced it as a juvenile, past, or irrelevant text. There is an obvious continuity in his understanding of religion from 1799 right through to his death in 1834.

NOTES

1   Schleiermacher, *On Religion*, 53.

2   G.W.F. Hegel, *Faith and Knowledge*, trans. Walter Cerf and H.S. Harris (Albany, NY: State University of New York Press,1977), 72.

3   G. W. F. Hegel, *The Difference between Fichte's and Schelling's System of Philosophy*, trans. H. S. Harris and W. Cerf (Albany: State University of New York Press, 1977), 83.

4   Cited in Richard Crouter, *Friedrich Schleiermacher, From Enlightenment to Romanticism* (Cambridge: Cambridge University Press: 2005), 91

5   Albert L. Blackwell, "The Antagonistic Correspondence of 1801 between Chaplain Sack and His Protégé Schleiermacher," *The Harvard Theological Review* 74, 1 (Jan., 1981): 101-121.

6   Blackwell, "The Antagonistic Correspondence": 111-112.

7   Blackwell, "The Antagonistic Correspondence": 113.

8   Stephen Neill, *The Interpretation of the New Testament: 1861-1961* (New York: Oxford University Press, 1966), 9-10.

MODULE 10
THE EVOLVING DEBATE

KEY POINTS

- The value of *On Religion* as a text today is chiefly historical.

- Rudolf Otto, Paul Tillich,* Martin Heidegger and Rudolf Bultmann are famous examples of scholars who have been inspired by the text.

- Schleiermacher's theory of religion has been taken up by feminist theologians and thinkers sympathetic to his anti-utilitarian politics.

Uses and Problems

Even in 1893, John Oman—who translated *On Religion* for publication in English—thought that the interest and value of the text "must now be chiefly historical." *On Religion* marks the transition, he wrote, from the Enlightenment "to the new time." The original text stands as a monument to the philosophical vision of the early German Romantics and to the author's urgency on the subject of religion in nineteenth-century Berlin.

Today, the importance of the text itself as a document continues to rest chiefly in its historical value. Nevertheless, the formative influence that Schleiermacher's portrayal of religion had on the field of Christian theology—certainly through *On Religion*, but even more so through the more comprehensive *Christian Faith*—is such that a number of later thinkers sought to challenge it. The Protestant theologians Karl Barth and Emil Brunner* were prominent among Schleiermacher's twentieth-century critics in his native Germany. They labeled Schleiermacher a liberal theologian in light of Ludwig Feuerbach's* critique of Christianity. This stated that theological claims express

> ❝ Schleiermacher is not dead for us and his theological work has not been transcended. If anyone still speaks today in Protestant theology as though he was still among us, it is Schleiermacher. We study Paul and the reformers, but we see with the eyes of Schleiermacher and think along the same lines as he did. ❞
>
> Karl Barth, *The Theology of Schleiermacher*

*anthropological** rather than theological truths—that is, they tell us something about what it means to be human.

While they respected his brilliant rhetorical force, Barth and Brunner were concerned that Schleiermacher's redefinition of religion for modernity collapsed belief in God into a description of some aspect of human consciousness. Indeed, Brunner argued that Schleiermacher had offered a "subjective interpretation" of the faith of the church, meaning that he emptied Christian faith of all content, making it simply about the inner emotional life of the individual believer. He wrote: "this great thinker who understood how to bring together Pietism, the Enlightenment, and Idealism into a most impressive unity, pointed the way to a distinctive feature of the nineteenth century—the subjective dissolution of theology."[1]

Karl Barth, meanwhile, argued that Schleiermacher's emphasis on human experience and feeling meant he failed to uphold the sovereignty of God. Schleiermacher, he reckoned, spoke of God "simply by speaking of man in a loud voice."[2]

Schools of Thought

By considering the influence *On Religion* has had on four major twentieth-century thinkers in particular, we can begin to get a flavor of its tremendous significance within the fields of theology and

philosophy. All four of these thinkers have drawn on Schleiermacher's ideas when developing new theories of their own.

Rudolf Otto (1869–1937) was a German Lutheran theologian and the editor of a special centenary edition of *On Religion*. In his most famous work, *The Idea of the Holy*, Otto expounds a concept of the holy or "numinous" that, being a "non-rational, non-sensory experience or feeling whose primary and immediate object is outside the self."[3] These are indebted to Schleiermacher's portrait of religious belief as non-cognitive and experiential.

Paul Tillich was a German theologian who incorporated both Otto's and Schleiermacher's work on religion into his own account of faith as an "Ultimate Concern," that transcends the structures of rational consciousness. Tillich was also inspired by Schleiermacher's teaching in *On Religion* that the Infinite cannot be conceived by the finite human intellect, but can only be intuited in the midst of the finite world. Portraying monotheistic religion as an encounter with the holy Other, Tillich stressed that Christian believers would be wrong to perceive God as if He were one half of an object-subject dichotomy. Martin Heidegger (1889–1976), a German philosopher and existentialist thinker, was also deeply impressed by Schleiermacher's view that religion is a form of intuition (*Anschauung*) or immediate, pre-reflective feeling. Influenced by the second speech of *On Religion* in particular, Heidegger developed his own concept of "Event" (*Ereignis*).[4] This "Event" comprises the moment of immediate perception where one beholds a finite thing "in relation to the Universe"—that is, one *experiences* it before the mind has judged or categorized it.

Lastly, the concept of "demythology" developed by the New Testament scholar Rudolf Bultmann (1884–1976) was also influenced by Schleiermacher's non-cognitive and experiential understanding of faith. When he claimed that modern theologians should "demythologize" Scripture, Bultmann was not only arguing that

Biblical truths should be understood existentially. He was also emphasizing that believers should not see the Bible as a book of historical proofs or teachings, but as a way of encountering the living Christ.

In Current Scholarship

In *On Religion,* Schleiermacher critiques the rationalism of contemporary German culture, and the tendency of its institutions toward larger-scale management schemes that were, in his eyes, harmfully utilitarian in nature. Here he was referring to large institutions that tended to treat people as the means to an end—as objects that are "useful" to it—without allowing them to properly flourish as individuals. This was the time when the modern research university was born in Germany—an institution created to deal with anxieties about an excess of scientific knowledge and to organize such information in a well-ordered manner.[5]

In this context, Schleiermacher's fourth speech in particular calls for a return to community-based values that are established intuitively. He ventures here that the true meaning of human society is sought through love, imagination and desire, rather than through the imposition of formal structures and conventions. This aspect of the text would have found favor with his Romantic friends who held similar views. In the present day, certain feminist thinkers, including the British theologian Daphne Hampson, have praised Schleiermacher's holistic and Romantic approach to political and social theory. Hampson is particularly interested in Schleiermacher's portrayal of human beings as inherently social, who need community in order to flourish as individuals.

While Schleiermacher's texts continue to be read, taught, and studied widely at university level in both Europe and the United States, his philosophical and theological approach continues, of course, to influence theological thought. American theologians Katherine

Sonderegger* and Brian Gerrish,* for instance, cite Schleiermacher as formative influences. Moreover, in her book *God and Difference*, the queer theologian Linn-Marie Tonstad refers positively to Schleiermacher's theological project as one that offers a potentially good and fruitful model of religion for groups who have been marginalized and oppressed. This is because Schleiermacher gestures to an Infinite—a divine—who is present to all believers, regardless of their status in society.

NOTES

1   Emil Brunner, *The Divine-Human Encounter*, trans. Amendus W. Loos (London, S.C.M. Press, 1944), 24-5.

2   Karl Barth, *The Word of God and the Word of Man*, trans. Douglas Horton (New York and Evansion: Harper and Row, Publishers, 1957), 195f.

3   Rudolf Otto, *The Idea of the Holy* (New York: Oxford University Press, 1958), 10-11.

4   See Alexander S. Jensen, 'The Influence of Schleiermacher's Second Speech "On Religion" on Heidegger's Concept of "Ereignis"', *The Review of Metaphysics* 61, No. 4 (Jun., 2008): 815-826.

5   See Chad Wellmon, *Organizing Enlightenment: Information Overload and the Invention of the Modern Research University* (Baltimore, Maryland: John Hopkins University Press, 2016).

IMPACT AND INFLUENCE TODAY

KEY POINTS

- Schleiermacher's position in *On Religion* is often portrayed as a regrettable and "liberal" turn in the history of Protestant thought.

- The scholars George Lindbeck* and Wayne Proudfoot* have offered analyses of Schleiermacher's argument in *On Religion.*

- The prevailing image of Schleiermacher in the Anglo-American context is that he is a liberal theologian.

Position

On Religion is a classic text in the history of Christian thought, foundational for the discipline of religious studies in the West and famous for its presentation of religion as pre-reflective feeling. Nevertheless, in the twenty-first century, theologians and scholars of religion continue to debate not only the meaning and implications of Schleiermacher's definition of religion in the text, but also its coherence and helpfulness on a theoretical level. What does it mean to root religion in *Anschauung* (intuition)?

In the previous module, the criticisms that twentieth-century theologians Barth and Brunner made of Schleiermacher were highlighted. Karl Barth's negative characterization of him as a liberal theologian, in danger of domesticating the divine, has had an especially formative impact on the way that Schleiermacher is read and received by both German and Anglo-American scholars. As an American theologian put it in the mid twentieth-century: "history has selected

> **❝** Schleiermacher does not belong to the theologians alone, nor have they been allowed to monopolize him, though it is true that theologians have paid much more sympathetic attention to his ethics and dialectics than have philosophers, and perhaps rightly so. **❞**
>
> Roger Hausheer, "Three Major Originators of the Concept of Verstehen: Vico, Herder, Schleiermacher"

Barth to be the most audible voice in our times through which the theology of Schleiermacher continues to speak."[1]

Accordingly, as another scholar assessed in 1977: "the almost standard interpretation of Schleiermacher" is to read him "as a psychological reductionist, a theologian who would derive Christian beliefs and their contents from the religious feelings of believers."[2] Schleiermacher's position in *On Religion* is thus regularly portrayed in an unfavorable light—as a regrettable and "liberal" turn in the history of Protestant thought, which required challenging and correcting by subsequent Protestant thinkers.

Interaction

Within the Anglo-American context, another scholar who has contributed to perceptions about Schleiermacher in the fields of theology and religious studies (and whose position on Schleiermacher reflects a broader trend in interpretation) is George Lindbeck. In his 1982 book *The Nature of Doctrine: Religion and Theology in a Postliberal Age*, Lindbeck characterized Schleiermacher as an "experiential-expressivist" theologian. This is Lindbeck's own term. He argues that "experiential-expressivist" thinkers "locate ultimately significant contact with whatever is finally important to religion in the pre-reflexive experiential depths of the self."[3] For Lindbeck, then, Schleiermacher internalizes religion and renders everything we might

call "external" in the religious life—teachings, rituals, practices, and places of worship—merely peripheral and unessential.

Crucially, what this means for Lindbeck is that Schleiermacher limits differences and similarities between different religious faith traditions to variations and convergences between "underlying feelings, attitudes, existential orientations and practices." There is, he writes, "thus at least the logical possibility that a Buddhist and a Christian might have basically the same faith, although expressed very differently." Schleiermacher, in Lindbeck's eyes, therefore seems to be suggesting that all religious traditions have at their core the same content or substance. They are just *expressed* differently, according to external factors including the time and place of the expression.

Similarly, in his 1985 text *Religious Experience*, American scholar Wayne Proudfoot characterized *On Religion* as "the most influential statement and defense of the autonomy of religious experience."[4] With this claim, Proudfoot was arguing that Schleiermacher rooted religion in feeling and intuition in order to shield it from moral analysis or scientific or psychological critique. In other words, he was suggesting Schleiermacher grounded religion in the depth of human experience, rather than church tradition or metaphysical claims.

The Continuing Debate

Through the influence of first Barth and Brunner in the early to mid-twentieth century, followed by the contributions of Proudfoot and Lindbeck in the late twentieth-century, the prevalent characterization of Schleiermacher in Anglo-American scholarship remains that of an individualist theologian, who reduces religious belief to a facet of human consciousness, or human self-expression. In the history books, Schleiermacher is for this reason seen as a "liberal" theologian, at the same time as having changed the course of Protestant thought in the West.

Despite the prevailing "individualistic" Anglo-American image of Schleiermacher, however, numerous scholars are currently working to correct this portrait, among them academics like Julia Lamm* and Jacqueline Mariña.* Their challenge is to stress the inherently social dimension to Schleiermacher's understanding of religion (a point that has never been forgotten in Schleiermacher's native Germany). It is also to maintain that, for Schleiermacher, the religious life is the highest mode of inhabiting the world, and that it is a life that cannot be grounded in rational principles or made sense of through systematic argumentation. Rather, it is a response to the revelation of the ungraspable Infinite, the "*Whence*" of all finite existence.

NOTES

1 Schleiermacher on Christ and Religion (London: SCM Press, 1964), 10.

2 Edward Farley, "Is Schleiermacher Passé?," *Christian Faith Seeking Historical Understanding: Essays in Honor of Jack Forstman*, eds., James Duke and Anthony Dunnavant (Macon, Georgia: Mercer University Press, 1977), 10.

3 George Lindbeck, *The Nature of Doctrine: Religion and Theology in a Postliberal Age* (London: SPCK, 1984), 21.

4 Wayne Proudfoot, *Religious Experience* (Berkeley: University of California Press, 1987), ·—•

MODULE 12
WHERE NEXT?

KEY POINTS

- Schleiermacher's fifth speech, comparing the world's religions, is a foundational document for the discipline of comparative religion.

- *On Religion* is still the focus of debate in international conferences and symposia in the fields of theology and religious studies.

- The text is a striking cultural artefact of early nineteenth-century Germany, and a monument to early German Romanticism.

Potential

In 2008, a leading group of Schleiermacher experts from Europe and North America came together for a conference entitled "Schleiermacher, the Study of Religion, and the Future of Theology." Their meeting was based on the notion that the German theologian's philosophical and theological work is indeed enduringly influential. A brief outline of one of their proposals regarding *On Religion* will help us to gauge the potential for further developing the text's core ideas.

German theologian Notger Slenczka* argued at the gathering that Schleiermacher's presentation of world religions in his fifth speech would be a helpful dialogue partner for "pluralistic theologies of religion." Schleiermacher's own view is that religious believers belonging to different faith traditions will never be able to discuss their respective religions truly objectively. Religions, he says, can only be properly grasped and known by someone who belongs to the religious

> **❝** In a time dominated by reactionary visions of religion, and especially of Christianity, a renewed emphasis upon the resources inherent to liberal theology in general, and Schleiermacher in particular, is much needed. **❞**
>
> Steven R. Jungkeit, *Spaces of Modern Theology: Geography and Power in Schleiermacher's World*

tradition in question. When Schleiermacher compares the faiths of the world in speech five, then, we find him conducting his analysis from the confessional perspective of the Christian faith, and in such a way that gives the Christian form of religion prime position over all other religious traditions.

For Slenczka, Schleiermacher's refusal to admit that any sort of "objective" comparison is possible presents a helpful challenge to theologians like John Hick and Reinhold Bernhardt. Their aim is to find a way of understanding religion that does not prioritize the truth claims or doctrines of one particular religious tradition over the rest. Yet if Schleiermacher's approach here is going to be taken up as a viable way forward for "pluralistic theologies of religion," then what must be taken into account is also Schleiermacher social and historical context, and his own prejudices against people of other ethnic, racial and religious groups. Indeed, there are aspects to Schleiermacher's exercise in comparative religion—including his depiction of Judaism as a "dead" religion—which are not fit for emulation or development in theology today. Not only do they display a lack of respect and justice on his part, but also a lack of knowledge about those groups to which he doesn't belong.

Future Directions

In 1996, The Schleiermacher Society was founded by a group of

German scholars from various academic disciplines (history, philosophy, religious studies, ethics and theology). Its founding members include Günter Meckenstock,* who is one of the chief editors of the critical edition of Schleiermacher's complete works. Based in Halle, where Schleiermacher studied, the society holds regular conferences and symposia on his work and connected themes. Schleiermacher is upheld as a thinker who marks the dawning of a new epoch in Protestant theology and whose work continues to challenge scholars working at the boundaries of a number of disciplines.

Schleiermacher's role in the history of modern religious thought— including his contribution to Biblical hermeneutics and to the definition of "religion" as a term we use to compare different religious traditions, as well as his distinctive understanding of religion as feeling—has come under scrutiny recently in a number of different international research projects. Scholars like Thomas Albert Howard* and Suzanne Marchand* have included Schleiermacher in their thinking about the history of the modern research university.

Between 2012-2017, a research project at the University of Cambridge looked at "Bible and Antiquity in Nineteenth-Century Culture," and considered Schleiermacher a key figure in their examination of the period. This historical interest in Schleiermacher's life and work, the contribution he made to the way theology is studied in German universities, his defense of academic and social freedoms, but also the negative role he played in the persistence of anti-Jewish feeling within the nineteenth-century university—all of these remain fertile topics for examination.

Summary

Because of its place in the history of modern religious thought, *On Religion* will remain a classic text and a standard work for study by undergraduates in the disciplines of religious studies and theology. It

remains relevant as a source text for modern philosophers and theologians who are interested in the discipline of comparative religion, the relationship between the Church and the state, the status of religion as "non-cognitive," Schleiermacher's liberal portrait of the human subject as an irreducibly unique individual, and the relationship between religion and aesthetic theory.

The text is also a striking literary artefact of early German Romanticism and reflects the status of religion as a waning force or influence among the intellectual elites in Enlightenment Berlin. The close of the eighteenth century marked the fulcrum of an extremely important period not only for German philosophy, literature and poetry (the impressive figures of Herder, Kant, Fichte, Goethe and Schelling loomed large at this point) but also for the development of modern scientific methodology. Through its ideas and its form, On Religion reveals this complex and ever-changing intellectual climate and testifies to Schleiermacher's unique position within its ferment: a participant in Enlightenment rationalism, early German Romanticism and the established Prussian Church.

GLOSSARY

GLOSSARY OF TERMS

Aesthetics: a branch of philosophy concerned with the nature of beauty, art, and judgement.

Anthropology: the study of human societies and cultures and their development.

Apologetics: conceived broadly, this is the practice of defending the truth and value of particular religious systems or doctrines through argumentation.

Bildung: a German word and concept often translated as "cultivation," "education" or "development."

Catechesis: the practice of teaching in the Christian Church, whereby believers–especially children–learn about the doctrines and practices of the Christian Faith.

Christology: a sub-discipline of Christian theology which considers the question "Who is Jesus Christ?," and expounds the teaching that Christ is the Son of God.

Civil rights: a class of rights that protect personal freedom and enable individuals to take part in the political life of the society and state without facing oppression or discrimination.

Comparative religion: a sub-discipline of religious studies concerned with comparing the different world religions, and exploring their approaches to teaching, worshipping, praxis, and organizational structure.

Determinism: a term which broadly characterizes the view that an event or happening is guaranteed to take place, given a certain set of conditions.

Dialectical method: a form of argumentation whereby philosophers approach a conclusion by setting up and contrasting two or more opposing viewpoints.

Early German Romanticism or Frühromantik (1797-1802): a group of philosophers, poets and theorists, including Friedrich Schleiermacher, Friedrich Schlegel and Novalis. The group sought to reinstate love, education, and art as central concerns in philosophical, ethical, and political thinking.

Enlightenment, or Age of Enlightenment: a Europe-wide intellectual movement of the late seventeenth and eighteenth centuries, which emphasized individual freedom and prioritized the role of reason in social and political life.

Existentialism: a philosophical movement characterized by the conviction that thinking about the universe and its nature must begin at the level of the individual.

The Frankfurt School: a group of theorists and philosophers founded in 1922, with a united interest in the work of Karl Marx and an ambition for social change. Major thinkers include Theodor Adorno, Franz Leopold Naumann, Jürgen Habermas and Walter Benjamin.

French Revolution (1789–1799): a period of social and political turmoil in France, which saw the French monarchy overthrown and a republic established. Following violent periods of political

unrest, the Revolution culminated with Napoleon Bonaparte becoming dictator of France.

Hermeneutics: the branch of academic enquiry that develops and evaluates different methods of interpretation, especially the interpretation of texts.

Historical Criticism: a method of reading texts which seeks to understand a given text in terms of its original context, and which involves researching the original author(s), their purposes, and the intended audience.

Liberal Theology: a wide and perhaps vague term, which describes dominating trends within Protestant theology in the nineteenth century, including the argument that theology should develop in response to advances in philosophy, the natural sciences and historical critical disciplines. Schleiermacher is often referred to as the "father of liberal theology."

Liberation Theology: a political movement which interprets Christian teaching firstly in regard to the question of human suffering, and secondly in relation to instances of unjust economic, political or social conditions. Key figures include Gustavo Gutiérrez and Leonardo Boff.

Lutheranism: a Protestant Christian denomination rooted in the theology of Martin Luther.

Materialism: a philosophical theory which states that matter and energy are the only things that exist.

Metaphysics: a branch of philosophy which explores questions about the most fundamental constituents of reality, and how these are related to each other.

Napoleonic Wars (1799–1815): a series of major conflicts fought between the French Empire and its allies, led by Napoleon I, and a number of European powers.

The Old Testament: the name given by Christians to the first part of the Christian Bible. The text is based on the Hebrew Bible or Tanakh—the canonical collection of Jewish scriptural texts.

Pantheism Controversy (c.1780–90): an important dispute between two groups of German scholars–represented by Friedrich Heinrich Jacobi and Moses Mendelssohn–about the implications of Spinoza's philosophy. Jacobi and his followers claimed that Spinoza's depiction of God and Nature was materialist, and was, in the end, equivalent to atheism. In contrast, Mendelssohn's group argued that Spinoza's pantheism was in no significant way different to a theistic account of the universe.

Pietism: a significant movement within Lutheran Protestantism, which began in the seventeenth century and emphasized individual piety and devoted study of the Bible.

Protestantism: a term applied from the sixteenth century onwards to those churches and denominations adhering to the Reformation and rejecting certain Roman Catholic doctrines, including those pertaining to the sacraments and to papal supremacy.

Prussia: a historical German-speaking state that originated in 1525, and folded in 1947 after the defeat of German armies in World War II.

The Prussian capital was first Königsberg, and then Berlin from 1701, and the state itself was—at its peak—the largest and most dominant in the German Empire.

Prussian Union of Churches: in 1817, this union brought the German Lutheran and Reformed Churches together into a single church, creating one of the largest Protestant church bodies in Europe. The union was brought about through a series of decrees issued by Frederick William III of Prussia, and was supported by Schleiermacher.

Psychological determinism: the view that it is a person's mental or psychological state–extending to their thoughts, desires, and intuitions–that determines the actions that he or she will perform.

Rationalism: a philosophical position according to which reason, rather than human experience or empirical data, is the primary source and test of knowledge. In the eighteenth century, rationalism was associated with a kind of politics which emphasized utilitarian government, freedom from religion, and rational choice.

Reformation, or Protestant Reformation: a schism which took place in Western Christianity in the sixteenth century. It was the culmination of numerous movements expressing discontent with church teaching, worship, and practices, but was made possible by the leadership of Martin Luther.

Reformed Church: a major denomination of churches within Protestant Christianity, whose practices and traditions are heavily influenced by the theology of Jean Calvin and other reformation-era theologians.

Religious Pluralism: an attitude whereby a number of religions and religious practices are understood to be valid and accepted as truthful to some extent.

Salon: a gathering of people—especially of writers and artists—at the house of a woman prominent in high society. While he was in Berlin between 1796–1806, Schleiermacher attended the gatherings of prominent salonières Henrietta Herz and Rahel Varnhagen.

The Storming of the Bastille: a violent assault on the Bastille—a political prison and fortress in the center of Paris—that took place in July 1789. It is recognized as the most volatile point of the French Revolution.

Sturm und Drang (Storm and Stress): a movement in German literature and poetry which emphasized the uniqueness of the human subject, and the human ability to feel and express deep emotion. Loosely tied to the period 1760–1785, its key figures included Johann Georg Hamann, H.L. Wagner and Johan Wolfgang von Goethe.

University of Halle: the university was founded in 1694 and became a center for Pietism within Prussia. Schleiermacher entered Halle first as a student (1787–1790) and then as university preacher and professor of theology (1803–6). In 1817, after Schleiermacher had left, the University of Halle merged with the University of Wittemberg, and is now known as the Martin Luther University of Halle-Wittenberg.

Utilitarianism: an ethical theory which holds that the goal in a given situation should be the maximization of overall happiness.

Weimar Classicism (1772 – 1805): a cultural and literary movement in Germany, which drew on motifs and ways of thinking associated with the Enlightenment, Romanticism, and with the modern reception of classical texts and ideas.

PEOPLE MENTIONED IN THE TEXT

Saint Augustine of Hippo (354–430) was a North African bishop and theologian who converted to Christianity through Neo-Platonism and wrote influentially on the nature of sin as "original," on the character of evil as a privation of goodness, and on the doctrine of creation out of nothing. He was of major importance for Aquinas, Anselm of Canterbury, and Bonaventura and his writings continue to be formative and authoritative for the Christian Tradition in the Latin West.

Karl Barth (1886–1968) was a Swiss Reformed theologian who emphasized divine transcendence and the radical nature of the revelation of God in Christ. Regarded as the most famous and influential theologian of the twentieth century, Barth deeply respected Schleiermacher but was also a major critic of his impact on Protestant thinking.

Marshall Berman (b. 1940) is an American philosopher, Marxist humanist and critic of modernity. His most notable work is *All That Is Solid Melts into Air*.

Emil Brunner (1889–1966) was a Swiss Reformed theologian and prominent critic of Schleiermacher. In his book *Mysticism and the Word*, Brunner argued that Schleiermacher grounded his theology in a conception of human identity that failed to uphold the authority of the gospel, and so God's word.

Martin Buber (1878–1965) was an Austrian Jewish philosopher and critic of modernity who privileged the study of relationships rather than concepts. He is the author of *I and Thou*.

Cicero (106BC–43BC) was one of the finest orators and prose writers in Ancient Rome, and a master of the Latin language. He was an inspiration to the revolutionaries behind the French Revolution and his work was widely read within philosophical circles in early nineteenth-century Europe.

Wilhelm Dilthey (1833–1911) was a German philosopher interested in hermeneutics and sociology. He was a renowned biographer of Schleiermacher and an influence on Martin Heidegger.

Johann Gottlieb Fichte (1762–1814) was a German philosopher and contributor to German Idealism, who was centrally-preoccupied with the issues of human self-consciousness and freedom. His works include *Foundations of Natural Right*, and *Doctrine of Science*.

Ludwig Feuerbach (1804–1872) was a German anthropologist, philosopher, and critic of Christianity. He argued that when theological claims are properly understood, they are recognized as expressing anthropological as opposed to theological truths.

Hans Georg Gadamer (1900–2002) was a German philosopher and Plato scholar. His book *Truth and Method* was a major contribution to modern philosophical hermeneutics and also established him as a nuanced critic of Schleiermacher.

Brian Gerrish is John Nuveen Professor Emeritus in the Divinity School of the University of Chicago and Distinguished Service Professor of Theology Seminary. He is the author of *A Prince of the Church: Schleiermacher and the Beginnings of Modern Theology*, among other important works.

Johann Wolfgang von Goethe (1749–1832), German poet, writer, and artist. His first novel *The Trials of Young Werther*, and his second– *Wilhelm Meister's Apprenticeship*–were important influences on Friedrich Schlegel and the early German Romantics.

Daphne Hampson (b. 1944) is a British theologian, feminist, and critic of the established church, for whom God is found in human religious experience. She is the author of *Theology and Feminism*, among other important works.

Georg Philipp Friedrich Freiherr von Hardenberg, or "Novalis" (1772–1801) was a poet and a member of the German Romantic circle who died very young. His most famous and critically acclaimed collection of poetry is his *Hymns to the Night*.

Martin Heidegger (1889–1976) was an influential German existentialist philosopher, interested in language, hermeneutics and the "question of Being." His most famous work is his early book *Being and Time*, in which he critiques Kantian ontology, preferring to take a phenomenological approach to questions of self, world, and death.

Georg Wilhelm Friedrich Hegel (1770–1831) was a major German Idealist philosopher who gave a teleological account of world history. Major works include *Phenomenology of Spirit* and *Science of Logic*.

Johann Gottfried Herder (1744–1803) was a German poet, philosopher, and member of the Sturm und Drang movement, which, against the background of European Enlightenment, prized freedom of expression and saw love and feeling as central to human flourishing.

Thomas Albert Howard is a Professor of History and the Humanities at Valparaiso University, Indiana. He is the author of *Religion and the Rise of Historicism*, among other important works.

Friedrich Heinrich Jacobi (1743–1819) was a German philosopher and vociferous critic of the Enlightenment movement for what he saw as its nihilistic and reductive tendencies. He emphasized the role of faith in contrast to reason, and informed Schleiermacher's understanding of Spinoza's philosophy.

Immanuel Kant (1724–1804) was a German philosopher whose thinking had a deep, formative impact on the history of modern philosophy. He argued that human reason generates the general laws of nature and legislates the moral law for itself, and human autonomy was thereby a central concept in his philosophy.

Søren Kierkegaard (1813–55) was a Danish philosopher who is considered to be the father of the existentialist tradition. Like Schleiermacher, he wrote at length on the nature of faith, love, and the quality of human relationships. Major works include *Either/Or* and *Fear and Trembling*.

Julia Lamm (b. 1961) is an American scholar of religious studies.

Gottfried Wilhelm Leibniz (1646–1716) was a German philosopher and mathematician credited with popularizing rationalistic approaches to philosophy in the seventeenth and eighteenth centuries. His works include *Discourse on Metaphysics and Monadology*.

George Lindbeck (1923–2018) was an American scholar of religion. His most important work was *The Nature of Doctrine: Religion and Theology in a Postliberal Age*.

Martin Luther (1483–1546) was a German monk and theologian, and a figure of central significance to the Protestant Reformation. A key concept in his theology was the doctrine of justification by faith. His major works include his commentaries on the books of Genesis and Galatians.

Suzanne L. Marchand (b. 1961) is an American intellectual and cultural historian of modern Europe. She is the author of *German Orientalism in the Age of Empire: Religion, Race, and Scholarship*, among other important works.

Jacqueline Mariña is an American scholar of religion. She is the author of "Where Have All the Monads Gone? Substance and Transcendental Freedom in Schleiermacher," among other important works.

Günter Meckenstock (b. 1948) is a German protestant theologian. He is one of the chief editors of the critical edition of Schleiermacher's complete works.

Moses Mendelssohn (1729–1786) was a Jewish philosopher who is credited with influencing the Haskalah, the Jewish Enlightenment of the late eighteenth century. Schleiermacher was close to his daughter, Dorothea Veit.

Maurice Merleau-Ponty (1908–61) was a French philosopher, interested in questions of phenomenology, existentialism, perception and embodied experience. He was a friend of Sartre, and his works include *Phenomenology of Perception* and *The Visible and the Invisible*.

Rudolf Otto (1869–1937) was a German theologian and philosopher. His most famous work is *The Idea of the Holy*. He

edited of an anniversary edition of *On Religion*, published in Germany in 1926.

Paul the Apostle, or Saint Paul (c.C.E.5–c.C.E.67) was a early Christian writer, theologian, and founder of a number of church communities. He understood his mission to be the preaching of the gospel of Christ to the gentiles—that is, to those who are not Jewish. Fourteen books of the New Testament have been attributed to him.

Wayne Proudfoot (b. 1939) is a Professor of Religion at Columbia University. He is the author of *William James And A Science Of Religions: Reexperiencing The Varieties Of Religious Experience*, among other important works.

Karl Rahner (1904–84) was a German Jesuit theologian, famous for his concept of the "anonymous Christian." His works include *Foundations of Christian Faith* and *Theological Investigations* (23 vols.).

Paul Ricoeur (1913–2005) was a French philosopher interested in hermeneutics, narrative, and phenomenology. His major works include *Time and Narrative* (3 vols.), *Memory, History, Forgetting,* and *Oneself as Another.*

Friedrich Samuel Gottfried Sack (1738–1817) was a German Reformed theologian. He was Schleiermacher's friend and mentor.

Friedrich Wilhelm Joseph von Schelling (1775–1854) was a German Idealist philosopher interested in the themes of knowledge, beauty and science. His major works include *Philosophy of Nature* and *System of Transcendental Idealism.*

Johann Christoph Friedrich von Schiller (1759–1805) was a German poet, philosopher and writer who was a friend of the playwright Goethe and a member of the influential Sturm und Drang movement. Notable works of his include his plays *William Tell* and *Mary Stuart*.

Karl Wilhelm Friedrich Schlegel (1772–1829) was a German poet, theorist, critic, philosopher, and member of the early German Romantic movement. He was a close friend of Schleiermacher's while the latter wrote *On Religion*, and the two had embarked on a project to translate Plato's dialogues into German.

Johann S. Semler (1725–1791) was a rationalist theologian and church historian. He was still a professor at the University of Halle when Schleiermacher was a student.

Notger Slenczka (b. 1960) is a German Protestant theologian. She is the author of "Religion and the Religions: The Fifth Speech in Dialogue with Contemporary Conceptions of a Theology of Religions," among other important works.

Katherine Sonderegger is an American systematic theologian. She is the William Meade Chair in Systematic Theology at Virginia Theological Seminary and the author of the *Doctrine of God*.

Benedict de Spinoza (1632–77) was an important proto-enlightenment philosopher and metaphysician who took a mathematical and systematic approach to investigating reality. Widely condemned as a pantheist, his most influential work was the posthumously published *Ethics*.

Paul Tillich (1886–1965) was a German-American philosopher and theologian who began his academic career in Berlin in 1919 and finished it at the University of Chicago, having held a professorship at Harvard University. His work was influenced by Schleiermacher's.

Linn Marie Tonstad is an American systematic theologian, who teaches Women's, Gender, and Sexuality Studies as well as LGBT Studies.

Dorothea Veit (1764–1839) was a German writer and translator, and daughter of Moses Mendelssohn. She belonged to the same Berlin circle of early German Romantics as Schleiermacher.

Theodore Vial is an American scholar of religion. He is the author of *Modern Religion, Modern Race*, among other important works.

Christian Wolff (1679–1754) was German rationalist philosopher known for his demonstrative, mathematical approach to problem-solving.

WORKS CITED

WORKS CITED

Barth, Karl. *The Word of God and the Word of Man*. Translated by Douglas Horton. New York and Evansion: Harper and Row, 1957.

Blackwell, Albert L. "The Antagonistic Correspondence of 1801 between Chaplain Sack and His Protégé Schleiermacher." *The Harvard Theological Review* 74, no 1. (Jan., 1981): 101-121.

Brunner, Emil. *The Divine-Human Encounter*. Translated by Amendus W. Loos. London, S.C.M. Press, 1944.

Beiser, Frederick. *The Romantic Imperative*. Cambridge, MA: Harvard University Press, 2003.

Crouter, Richard. *Friedrich Schleiermacher, From Enlightenment to Romanticism*. Cambridge: Cambridge University Press: 2005.

Dilthey, Wilhelm. *Selected Writings*. Translated by H. P. Rickman, Cambridge: Cambridge University Press, 1976.

Farley, Edward. "Is Schleiermacher Passé?". In *Christian Faith Seeking Historical Understanding: Essays in Honor of Jack Forstman*, edited by James Duke and Anthony Dunnavant, 9-27. Macon, Georgia: Mercer University Press, 1977.

Forstman, Jack. *A Romantic Triangle: Schleiermacher and Early German Romanticism*. Missoula, MT: Scholars Press, 1977.

Friedländer, David, Schleiermacher, Friedrich and Teller, Wilhelm Abraham. *A Debate on Jewish Emancipation and Christian Theology in Old Berlin*. Edited by Richard Crouter and Julie Klassen. Indianapolis/Cambridge: Hackett Publishing Company, 2004.

Friess, Horace Leland, trans. *Schleiermacher's Soliloquies: An English Translation of the Monologen with a Critical Introduction and Appendix*. Chicago: Open Court Pub. Co., 1926.

Gerrish, B. A. *A Prince of the Church: Schleiermacher and the Beginnings of Modern Theology*. Philadelphia, PA: Fortress Press, 1984.

Hausheer, Roger. 'Three Major Originators of the Concept of Verstehen: Vico, Herder, and Schleiermacher', in *Verstehen and Humane Understanding*, edited by Anthony O'Hear, pp. 47-72. Cambridge: Cambridge University, 1996.

Hegel, G.W.F. *Faith and Knowledge*. Translated by Walter Cerf and H.S. Harris. Albany, NY: State University of New York Press,1977.

Hegel, G. W. F. *The Difference between Fichte's and Schelling's System of Philosophy.* Translated by H. S. Harris and W. Cerf. Albany: State University of New York Press, 1977.

Jensen, Alexander S. 'The Influence of Schleiermacher's Second Speech "On Religion" on Heidegger's Concept of "Ereignis"'. *The Review of Metaphysics* 61, No. 4 (June 2008): 815-826.

Jonas, Ludwig and Dilthey, Wilhelm, eds. *Aus Schleiermacher's Leben in Briefen*, Vol 1. Berlin: Reimer, 1860-1863.

Jungkeit, Steven R. *Spaces of Modern Theology: Geography and Power in Schleiermacher's World.* New York: Palgrave Macmillan, 2012.

Kwok, Pui-lan. *Postcolonial Imagination and Feminist Theology.* Louisville, KY: Westminter/John Knox Press, 2005.

Lindbeck, George. *The Nature of Doctrine: Religion and Theology in a Postliberal Age*, London: SPCK, 1984.

Neill, Stephen. *The Interpretation of the New Testament: 1861-1961.* New York: Oxford Univ. Press, 1966.

Otto, Rudolf. *The Idea of the Holy.* New York: Oxford University Press, 1958.

Proudfoot, Wayne. *Religious Experience.* Berkeley: University of California Press, 1987.

Quash, Ben. "Revelation". In *The Oxford Handbook of Systematic Theology*, edited by John Webster, Kathryn Tanner, and Iain Torrance, 325-344. Oxford: Oxford University Press, 2007.

Schiller, Friedrich. *Schillers Werke. Nationalausgabe.* Edited by Eberhard Haufe, 43 Vols. Weimar: 1943–.

Schleiermacher, Friedrich. *Christian Faith* Translated by Terrence Tice, Catherine L. Kelsey, and Edwina Lawler. Louisville, KY: Westminster John Knox Press, 2016.

Schleiermacher, Friedrich. *On Religion: Speeches to Its Cultured Despisers*. Translated by John Oman. New York: Harper and Row, 1958.

Schleiermacher, Friedrich. *The Life of Schleiermacher: As Unfolded in His Autobiography and Letters*. Translated by Frederica Rowan. 2 vols. London: Smith, Elder and Co., 1860.

Schleiermacher, Friedrich. *Schleiermacher: On Religion: Speeches to Its Cultured Despisers.* Edited by Richard Crouter. Translated by Richard Crouter. Cambridge: Cambridge University Press, 1996.

Schlegel, Friedrich. *Friedrich Schlegel's Lucinde and the Fragments*. Translated by Peter Firchow Minneapolis: University of Minnesota Press, 1971.

Silz, Walter. *Early German Romanticism: Its Founders and Heinrich von Kleist*. Cambridge, Massachusetts: Harvard University Press, 1929.

Sockness, Brent W., and Wilhelm Gräb. *Schleiermacher, the Study of Religion, and the Future of Theology: A Transatlantic Dialogue*. Berlin: Walter de Gruyter, 2009.

Vander Schel, Kevin. *Embedded Grace: Christ, History, and the Reign of God in Schleiermacher's Dogmatics*. Philadelphia: Fortress Press, 2013.

Vial, Theodore. *Modern Religion, Modern Race*. Oxford: Oxford University Press, 2016.

THE MACAT LIBRARY
BY DISCIPLINE

AFRICANA STUDIES

Chinua Achebe's *An Image of Africa: Racism in Conrad's Heart of Darkness*
W. E. B. Du Bois's *The Souls of Black Folk*
Zora Neale Huston's *Characteristics of Negro Expression*
Martin Luther King Jr's *Why We Can't Wait*
Toni Morrison's *Playing in the Dark: Whiteness in the American Literary Imagination*

ANTHROPOLOGY

Arjun Appadurai's *Modernity at Large: Cultural Dimensions of Globalisation*
Philippe Ariès's *Centuries of Childhood*
Franz Boas's *Race, Language and Culture*
Kim Chan & Renée Mauborgne's *Blue Ocean Strategy*
Jared Diamond's *Guns, Germs & Steel: the Fate of Human Societies*
Jared Diamond's *Collapse: How Societies Choose to Fail or Survive*
E. E. Evans-Pritchard's *Witchcraft, Oracles and Magic Among the Azande*
James Ferguson's *The Anti-Politics Machine*
Clifford Geertz's *The Interpretation of Cultures*
David Graeber's *Debt: the First 5000 Years*
Karen Ho's *Liquidated: An Ethnography of Wall Street*
Geert Hofstede's *Culture's Consequences: Comparing Values, Behaviors, Institutes and Organizations across Nations*
Claude Lévi-Strauss's *Structural Anthropology*
Jay Macleod's *Ain't No Makin' It: Aspirations and Attainment in a Low-Income Neighborhood*
Saba Mahmood's *The Politics of Piety: The Islamic Revival and the Feminist Subject*
Marcel Mauss's *The Gift*

BUSINESS

Jean Lave & Etienne Wenger's *Situated Learning*
Theodore Levitt's *Marketing Myopia*
Burton G. Malkiel's *A Random Walk Down Wall Street*
Douglas McGregor's *The Human Side of Enterprise*
Michael Porter's *Competitive Strategy: Creating and Sustaining Superior Performance*
John Kotter's *Leading Change*
C. K. Prahalad & Gary Hamel's *The Core Competence of the Corporation*

CRIMINOLOGY

Michelle Alexander's *The New Jim Crow: Mass Incarceration in the Age of Colorblindness*
Michael R. Gottfredson & Travis Hirschi's *A General Theory of Crime*
Richard Herrnstein & Charles A. Murray's *The Bell Curve: Intelligence and Class Structure in American Life*
Elizabeth Loftus's *Eyewitness Testimony*
Jay Macleod's *Ain't No Makin' It: Aspirations and Attainment in a Low-Income Neighborhood*
Philip Zimbardo's *The Lucifer Effect*

ECONOMICS

Janet Abu-Lughod's *Before European Hegemony*
Ha-Joon Chang's *Kicking Away the Ladder*
David Brion Davis's *The Problem of Slavery in the Age of Revolution*
Milton Friedman's *The Role of Monetary Policy*
Milton Friedman's *Capitalism and Freedom*
David Graeber's *Debt: the First 5000 Years*
Friedrich Hayek's *The Road to Serfdom*
Karen Ho's *Liquidated: An Ethnography of Wall Street*

John Maynard Keynes's *The General Theory of Employment, Interest and Money*
Charles P. Kindleberger's *Manias, Panics and Crashes*
Robert Lucas's *Why Doesn't Capital Flow from Rich to Poor Countries?*
Burton G. Malkiel's *A Random Walk Down Wall Street*
Thomas Robert Malthus's *An Essay on the Principle of Population*
Karl Marx's *Capital*
Thomas Piketty's *Capital in the Twenty-First Century*
Amartya Sen's *Development as Freedom*
Adam Smith's *The Wealth of Nations*
Nassim Nicholas Taleb's *The Black Swan: The Impact of the Highly Improbable*
Amos Tversky's & Daniel Kahneman's *Judgment under Uncertainty: Heuristics and Biases*
Mahbub Ul Haq's *Reflections on Human Development*
Max Weber's *The Protestant Ethic and the Spirit of Capitalism*

FEMINISM AND GENDER STUDIES

Judith Butler's *Gender Trouble*
Simone De Beauvoir's *The Second Sex*
Michel Foucault's *History of Sexuality*
Betty Friedan's *The Feminine Mystique*
Saba Mahmood's *The Politics of Piety: The Islamic Revival and the Feminist Subject*
Joan Wallach Scott's *Gender and the Politics of History*
Mary Wollstonecraft's *A Vindication of the Rights of Woman*
Virginia Woolf's *A Room of One's Own*

GEOGRAPHY

The Brundtland Report's *Our Common Future*
Rachel Carson's *Silent Spring*
Charles Darwin's *On the Origin of Species*
James Ferguson's *The Anti-Politics Machine*
Jane Jacobs's *The Death and Life of Great American Cities*
James Lovelock's *Gaia: A New Look at Life on Earth*
Amartya Sen's *Development as Freedom*
Mathis Wackernagel & William Rees's *Our Ecological Footprint*

HISTORY

Janet Abu-Lughod's *Before European Hegemony*
Benedict Anderson's *Imagined Communities*
Bernard Bailyn's *The Ideological Origins of the American Revolution*
Hanna Batatu's *The Old Social Classes And The Revolutionary Movements Of Iraq*
Christopher Browning's *Ordinary Men: Reserve Police Batallion 101 and the Final Solution in Poland*
Edmund Burke's *Reflections on the Revolution in France*
William Cronon's *Nature's Metropolis: Chicago And The Great West*
Alfred W. Crosby's *The Columbian Exchange*
Hamid Dabashi's *Iran: A People Interrupted*
David Brion Davis's *The Problem of Slavery in the Age of Revolution*
Nathalie Zemon Davis's *The Return of Martin Guerre*
Jared Diamond's *Guns, Germs & Steel: the Fate of Human Societies*
Frank Dikotter's *Mao's Great Famine*
John W Dower's *War Without Mercy: Race And Power In The Pacific War*
W. E. B. Du Bois's *The Souls of Black Folk*
Richard J. Evans's *In Defence of History*
Lucien Febvre's *The Problem of Unbelief in the 16th Century*
Sheila Fitzpatrick's *Everyday Stalinism*

Eric Foner's *Reconstruction: America's Unfinished Revolution, 1863-1877*
Michel Foucault's *Discipline and Punish*
Michel Foucault's *History of Sexuality*
Francis Fukuyama's *The End of History and the Last Man*
John Lewis Gaddis's *We Now Know: Rethinking Cold War History*
Ernest Gellner's *Nations and Nationalism*
Eugene Genovese's *Roll, Jordan, Roll: The World the Slaves Made*
Carlo Ginzburg's *The Night Battles*
Daniel Goldhagen's *Hitler's Willing Executioners*
Jack Goldstone's *Revolution and Rebellion in the Early Modern World*
Antonio Gramsci's *The Prison Notebooks*
Alexander Hamilton, John Jay & James Madison's *The Federalist Papers*
Christopher Hill's *The World Turned Upside Down*
Carole Hillenbrand's *The Crusades: Islamic Perspectives*
Thomas Hobbes's *Leviathan*
Eric Hobsbawm's *The Age Of Revolution*
John A. Hobson's *Imperialism: A Study*
Albert Hourani's *History of the Arab Peoples*
Samuel P. Huntington's *The Clash of Civilizations and the Remaking of World Order*
C. L. R. James's *The Black Jacobins*
Tony Judt's *Postwar: A History of Europe Since 1945*
Ernst Kantorowicz's *The King's Two Bodies: A Study in Medieval Political Theology*
Paul Kennedy's *The Rise and Fall of the Great Powers*
Ian Kershaw's *The "Hitler Myth": Image and Reality in the Third Reich*
John Maynard Keynes's *The General Theory of Employment, Interest and Money*
Charles P. Kindleberger's *Manias, Panics and Crashes*
Martin Luther King Jr's *Why We Can't Wait*
Henry Kissinger's *World Order: Reflections on the Character of Nations and the Course of History*
Thomas Kuhn's *The Structure of Scientific Revolutions*
Georges Lefebvre's *The Coming of the French Revolution*
John Locke's *Two Treatises of Government*
Niccolò Machiavelli's *The Prince*
Thomas Robert Malthus's *An Essay on the Principle of Population*
Mahmood Mamdani's *Citizen and Subject: Contemporary Africa And The Legacy Of Late Colonialism*
Karl Marx's *Capital*
Stanley Milgram's *Obedience to Authority*
John Stuart Mill's *On Liberty*
Thomas Paine's *Common Sense*
Thomas Paine's *Rights of Man*
Geoffrey Parker's *Global Crisis: War, Climate Change and Catastrophe in the Seventeenth Century*
Jonathan Riley-Smith's *The First Crusade and the Idea of Crusading*
Jean-Jacques Rousseau's *The Social Contract*
Joan Wallach Scott's *Gender and the Politics of History*
Theda Skocpol's *States and Social Revolutions*
Adam Smith's *The Wealth of Nations*
Timothy Snyder's *Bloodlands: Europe Between Hitler and Stalin*
Sun Tzu's *The Art of War*
Keith Thomas's *Religion and the Decline of Magic*
Thucydides's *The History of the Peloponnesian War*
Frederick Jackson Turner's *The Significance of the Frontier in American History*
Odd Arne Westad's *The Global Cold War: Third World Interventions And The Making Of Our Times*

LITERATURE

Chinua Achebe's *An Image of Africa: Racism in Conrad's Heart of Darkness*
Roland Barthes's *Mythologies*
Homi K. Bhabha's *The Location of Culture*
Judith Butler's *Gender Trouble*
Simone De Beauvoir's *The Second Sex*
Ferdinand De Saussure's *Course in General Linguistics*
T. S. Eliot's *The Sacred Wood: Essays on Poetry and Criticism*
Zora Neale Huston's *Characteristics of Negro Expression*
Toni Morrison's *Playing in the Dark: Whiteness in the American Literary Imagination*
Edward Said's *Orientalism*
Gayatri Chakravorty Spivak's *Can the Subaltern Speak?*
Mary Wollstonecraft's *A Vindication of the Rights of Women*
Virginia Woolf's *A Room of One's Own*

PHILOSOPHY

Elizabeth Anscombe's *Modern Moral Philosophy*
Hannah Arendt's *The Human Condition*
Aristotle's *Metaphysics*
Aristotle's *Nicomachean Ethics*
Edmund Gettier's *Is Justified True Belief Knowledge?*
Georg Wilhelm Friedrich Hegel's *Phenomenology of Spirit*
David Hume's *Dialogues Concerning Natural Religion*
David Hume's *The Enquiry for Human Understanding*
Immanuel Kant's *Religion within the Boundaries of Mere Reason*
Immanuel Kant's *Critique of Pure Reason*
Søren Kierkegaard's *The Sickness Unto Death*
Søren Kierkegaard's *Fear and Trembling*
C. S. Lewis's *The Abolition of Man*
Alasdair MacIntyre's *After Virtue*
Marcus Aurelius's *Meditations*
Friedrich Nietzsche's *On the Genealogy of Morality*
Friedrich Nietzsche's *Beyond Good and Evil*
Plato's *Republic*
Plato's *Symposium*
Jean-Jacques Rousseau's *The Social Contract*
Gilbert Ryle's *The Concept of Mind*
Baruch Spinoza's *Ethics*
Sun Tzu's *The Art of War*
Ludwig Wittgenstein's *Philosophical Investigations*

POLITICS

Benedict Anderson's *Imagined Communities*
Aristotle's *Politics*
Bernard Bailyn's *The Ideological Origins of the American Revolution*
Edmund Burke's *Reflections on the Revolution in France*
John C. Calhoun's *A Disquisition on Government*
Ha-Joon Chang's *Kicking Away the Ladder*
Hamid Dabashi's *Iran: A People Interrupted*
Hamid Dabashi's *Theology of Discontent: The Ideological Foundation of the Islamic Revolution in Iran*
Robert Dahl's *Democracy and its Critics*
Robert Dahl's *Who Governs?*
David Brion Davis's *The Problem of Slavery in the Age of Revolution*

Alexis De Tocqueville's *Democracy in America*
James Ferguson's *The Anti-Politics Machine*
Frank Dikotter's *Mao's Great Famine*
Sheila Fitzpatrick's *Everyday Stalinism*
Eric Foner's *Reconstruction: America's Unfinished Revolution, 1863-1877*
Milton Friedman's *Capitalism and Freedom*
Francis Fukuyama's *The End of History and the Last Man*
John Lewis Gaddis's *We Now Know: Rethinking Cold War History*
Ernest Gellner's *Nations and Nationalism*
David Graeber's *Debt: the First 5000 Years*
Antonio Gramsci's *The Prison Notebooks*
Alexander Hamilton, John Jay & James Madison's *The Federalist Papers*
Friedrich Hayek's *The Road to Serfdom*
Christopher Hill's *The World Turned Upside Down*
Thomas Hobbes's *Leviathan*
John A. Hobson's *Imperialism: A Study*
Samuel P. Huntington's *The Clash of Civilizations and the Remaking of World Order*
Tony Judt's *Postwar: A History of Europe Since 1945*
David C. Kang's *China Rising: Peace, Power and Order in East Asia*
Paul Kennedy's *The Rise and Fall of Great Powers*
Robert Keohane's *After Hegemony*
Martin Luther King Jr.'s *Why We Can't Wait*
Henry Kissinger's *World Order: Reflections on the Character of Nations and the Course of History*
John Locke's *Two Treatises of Government*
Niccolò Machiavelli's *The Prince*
Thomas Robert Malthus's *An Essay on the Principle of Population*
Mahmood Mamdani's *Citizen and Subject: Contemporary Africa And The Legacy Of Late Colonialism*
Karl Marx's *Capital*
John Stuart Mill's *On Liberty*
John Stuart Mill's *Utilitarianism*
Hans Morgenthau's *Politics Among Nations*
Thomas Paine's *Common Sense*
Thomas Paine's *Rights of Man*
Thomas Piketty's *Capital in the Twenty-First Century*
Robert D. Putman's *Bowling Alone*
John Rawls's *Theory of Justice*
Jean-Jacques Rousseau's *The Social Contract*
Theda Skocpol's *States and Social Revolutions*
Adam Smith's *The Wealth of Nations*
Sun Tzu's *The Art of War*
Henry David Thoreau's *Civil Disobedience*
Thucydides's *The History of the Peloponnesian War*
Kenneth Waltz's *Theory of International Politics*
Max Weber's *Politics as a Vocation*
Odd Arne Westad's *The Global Cold War: Third World Interventions And The Making Of Our Times*

POSTCOLONIAL STUDIES

Roland Barthes's *Mythologies*
Frantz Fanon's *Black Skin, White Masks*
Homi K. Bhabha's *The Location of Culture*
Gustavo Gutiérrez's *A Theology of Liberation*
Edward Said's *Orientalism*
Gayatri Chakravorty Spivak's *Can the Subaltern Speak?*

PSYCHOLOGY

Gordon Allport's *The Nature of Prejudice*
Alan Baddeley & Graham Hitch's *Aggression: A Social Learning Analysis*
Albert Bandura's *Aggression: A Social Learning Analysis*
Leon Festinger's *A Theory of Cognitive Dissonance*
Sigmund Freud's *The Interpretation of Dreams*
Betty Friedan's *The Feminine Mystique*
Michael R. Gottfredson & Travis Hirschi's *A General Theory of Crime*
Eric Hoffer's *The True Believer: Thoughts on the Nature of Mass Movements*
William James's *Principles of Psychology*
Elizabeth Loftus's *Eyewitness Testimony*
A. H. Maslow's *A Theory of Human Motivation*
Stanley Milgram's *Obedience to Authority*
Steven Pinker's *The Better Angels of Our Nature*
Oliver Sacks's *The Man Who Mistook His Wife For a Hat*
Richard Thaler & Cass Sunstein's *Nudge: Improving Decisions About Health, Wealth and Happiness*
Amos Tversky's *Judgment under Uncertainty: Heuristics and Biases*
Philip Zimbardo's *The Lucifer Effect*

SCIENCE

Rachel Carson's *Silent Spring*
William Cronon's *Nature's Metropolis: Chicago And The Great West*
Alfred W. Crosby's *The Columbian Exchange*
Charles Darwin's *On the Origin of Species*
Richard Dawkin's *The Selfish Gene*
Thomas Kuhn's *The Structure of Scientific Revolutions*
Geoffrey Parker's *Global Crisis: War, Climate Change and Catastrophe in the Seventeenth Century*
Mathis Wackernagel & William Rees's *Our Ecological Footprint*

SOCIOLOGY

Michelle Alexander's *The New Jim Crow: Mass Incarceration in the Age of Colorblindness*
Gordon Allport's *The Nature of Prejudice*
Albert Bandura's *Aggression: A Social Learning Analysis*
Hanna Batatu's *The Old Social Classes And The Revolutionary Movements Of Iraq*
Ha-Joon Chang's *Kicking Away the Ladder*
W. E. B. Du Bois's *The Souls of Black Folk*
Émile Durkheim's *On Suicide*
Frantz Fanon's *Black Skin, White Masks*
Frantz Fanon's *The Wretched of the Earth*
Eric Foner's *Reconstruction: America's Unfinished Revolution, 1863-1877*
Eugene Genovese's *Roll, Jordan, Roll: The World the Slaves Made*
Jack Goldstone's *Revolution and Rebellion in the Early Modern World*
Antonio Gramsci's *The Prison Notebooks*
Richard Herrnstein & Charles A Murray's *The Bell Curve: Intelligence and Class Structure in American Life*
Eric Hoffer's *The True Believer: Thoughts on the Nature of Mass Movements*
Jane Jacobs's *The Death and Life of Great American Cities*
Robert Lucas's *Why Doesn't Capital Flow from Rich to Poor Countries?*
Jay Macleod's *Ain't No Makin' It: Aspirations and Attainment in a Low Income Neighborhood*
Elaine May's *Homeward Bound: American Families in the Cold War Era*
Douglas McGregor's *The Human Side of Enterprise*
C. Wright Mills's *The Sociological Imagination*

Thomas Piketty's *Capital in the Twenty-First Century*
Robert D. Putman's *Bowling Alone*
David Riesman's *The Lonely Crowd: A Study of the Changing American Character*
Edward Said's *Orientalism*
Joan Wallach Scott's *Gender and the Politics of History*
Theda Skocpol's *States and Social Revolutions*
Max Weber's *The Protestant Ethic and the Spirit of Capitalism*

THEOLOGY

Augustine's *Confessions*
Benedict's *Rule of St Benedict*
Gustavo Gutiérrez's *A Theology of Liberation*
Carole Hillenbrand's *The Crusades: Islamic Perspectives*
David Hume's *Dialogues Concerning Natural Religion*
Immanuel Kant's *Religion within the Boundaries of Mere Reason*
Ernst Kantorowicz's *The King's Two Bodies: A Study in Medieval Political Theology*
Søren Kierkegaard's *The Sickness Unto Death*
C. S. Lewis's *The Abolition of Man*
Saba Mahmood's *The Politics of Piety: The Islamic Revival and the Feminist Subject*
Baruch Spinoza's *Ethics*
Keith Thomas's *Religion and the Decline of Magic*

Macat Disciplines

Access the greatest ideas and thinkers across entire disciplines, including

AFRICANA STUDIES

Chinua Achebe's *An Image of Africa:*
Racism in Conrad's Heart of Darkness

W. E. B. Du Bois's *The Souls of Black Folk*

Zora Neale Hurston's *Characteristics of Negro Expression*

Martin Luther King Jr.'s *Why We Can't Wait*

Toni Morrison's *Playing in the Dark:*
Whiteness in the American Literary Imagination

Macat analyses are available from all good bookshops and libraries.

Access hundreds of analyses through one, multimedia tool.
Join free for one month **library.macat.com**

Macat Disciplines

Access the greatest ideas and thinkers across entire disciplines, including

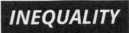

INEQUALITY

Ha-Joon Chang's, *Kicking Away the Ladder*

David Graeber's, *Debt: The First 5000 Years*

Robert E. Lucas's, *Why Doesn't Capital Flow from Rich To Poor Countries?*

Thomas Piketty's, *Capital in the Twenty-First Century*

Amartya Sen's, *Inequality Re-Examined*

Mahbub Ul Haq's, *Reflections on Human Development*

Macat Disciplines

Access the greatest ideas and thinkers across entire disciplines, including

CRIMINOLOGY

Michelle Alexander's
*The New Jim Crow:
Mass Incarceration in the
Age of Colorblindness*

**Michael R. Gottfredson
& Travis Hirschi's**
A General Theory of Crime

Elizabeth Loftus's
Eyewitness Testimony

**Richard Herrnstein
& Charles A. Murray's**
*The Bell Curve: Intelligence and
Class Structure in American Life*

Jay Macleod's
*Ain't No Makin' It:
Aspirations and Attainment in a
Low-Income Neighborhood*

Philip Zimbardo's
The Lucifer Effect

Macat analyses are available from all good bookshops and libraries.

Access hundreds of analyses through one, multimedia tool.
Join free for one month **library.macat.com**

Macat Disciplines

Access the greatest ideas and thinkers across entire disciplines, including

Postcolonial Studies

Roland Barthes's *Mythologies*
Frantz Fanon's *Black Skin, White Masks*
Homi K. Bhabha's *The Location of Culture*
Gustavo Gutiérrez's *A Theology of Liberation*
Edward Said's *Orientalism*
Gayatri Chakravorty Spivak's *Can the Subaltern Speak?*

Macat Disciplines

Access the greatest ideas and thinkers across entire disciplines, including

Macat Pairs

Analyse historical and modern issues from opposite sides of an argument. Pairs include:

ARE WE FUNDAMENTALLY GOOD - OR BAD?

Steven Pinker's
The Better Angels of Our Nature

Stephen Pinker's gloriously optimistic 2011 book argues that, despite humanity's biological tendency toward violence, we are, in fact, less violent today than ever before. To prove his case, Pinker lays out pages of detailed statistical evidence. For him, much of the credit for the decline goes to the eighteenth-century Enlightenment movement, whose ideas of liberty, tolerance, and respect for the value of human life filtered down through society and affected how people thought. That psychological change led to behavioral change—and overall we became more peaceful. Critics countered that humanity could never overcome the biological urge toward violence; others argued that Pinker's statistics were flawed.

Philip Zimbardo's
The Lucifer Effect

Some psychologists believe those who commit cruelty are innately evil. Zimbardo disagrees. In *The Lucifer Effect*, he argues that sometimes good people do evil things simply because of the situations they find themselves in, citing many historical examples to illustrate his point. Zimbardo details his 1971 Stanford prison experiment, where ordinary volunteers playing guards in a mock prison rapidly became abusive. But he also describes the tortures committed by US army personnel in Iraq's Abu Ghraib prison in 2003—and how he himself testified in defence of one of those guards. committed by US army personnel in Iraq's Abu Ghraib prison in 2003—and how he himself testified in defence of one of those guards.

Macat analyses are available from all good bookshops and libraries.

Access hundreds of analyses through one, multimedia tool.
Join free for one month **library.macat.com**

Macat Pairs

Analyse historical and modern issues from opposite sides of an argument. Pairs include:

HOW WE RELATE TO EACH OTHER AND SOCIETY

Jean-Jacques Rousseau's
The Social Contract

Rousseau's famous work sets out the radical concept of the 'social contract': a give-and-take relationship between individual freedom and social order.

If people are free to do as they like, governed only by their own sense of justice, they are also vulnerable to chaos and violence. To avoid this, Rousseau proposes, they should agree to give up some freedom to benefit from the protection of social and political organization. But this deal is only just if societies are led by the collective needs and desires of the people, and able to control the private interests of individuals. For Rousseau, the only legitimate form of government is rule by the people.

Robert D. Putnam's
Bowling Alone

In *Bowling Alone*, Robert Putnam argues that Americans have become disconnected from one another and from the institutions of their common life, and investigates the consequences of this change.

Looking at a range of indicators, from membership in formal organizations to the number of invitations being extended to informal dinner parties, Putnam demonstrates that Americans are interacting less and creating less "social capital" – with potentially disastrous implications for their society.

It would be difficult to overstate the impact of *Bowling Alone*, one of the most frequently cited social science publications of the last half-century.

Macat analyses are available from all good bookshops and libraries.

Access hundreds of analyses through one, multimedia tool.
Join free for one month **library.macat.com**